Enoch Fitch Burr

Celestial Empires

Enoch Fitch Burr

Celestial Empires

ISBN/EAN: 9783337172169

Printed in Europe, USA, Canada, Australia, Japan

Cover: Foto ©ninafisch / pixelio.de

More available books at **www.hansebooks.com**

CELESTIAL EMPIRES.

BY

REV. E. F. BURR, D. D.,

AUTHOR OF "ECCE CŒLUM," "AD FIDEM," "PATER MUNDI,"
"TEMPTED TO UNBELIEF," ETC.

AMERICAN TRACT SOCIETY,
150 NASSAU STREET, NEW YORK.

COPYRIGHT, 1885,

BY AMERICAN TRACT SOCIETY.

PROJECTIONS FROM THE SUN'S PHOTOSPHERE.

PREFACE.

Sir Isaac Newton inserted a religious scholium in the heart of his "Principia."

Louis Agassiz, on opening a session in Biology on the island of Penikese, said to his class, "Young gentlemen, before we commence to look into the secrets of nature let us seek wisdom from nature's God. Let us pray."

The most eloquent expounder of science in this country during the last generation wrote at the close of his long and brilliant professional career, "I can truly declare that in the study and exhibitions of science to my pupils and fellowmen I have never forgotten to give all honor and glory to the infinite Creator—happy if I might be the honored interpreter of a portion of his works and of the beautiful structure and beneficent laws discovered therein by the labors of many illustrious predecessors. For this I claim no credit. It is the result to which right reason and sound philosophy, as well as religion, would naturally lead."

Was such a "mixing up" of religion with

PREFACE.

science in good taste? Was it *scientific?* Some say, No, and say it loudly. "The two things differ so widely in their natures. They belong to such different realms. They aim at such different objects. They pursue their objects by such different roads. Who has not heard of the 'scientific method,' and who does not know that it differs by whole diameters from the method of faith? Let the two poles keep apart. It will be for the comfort and advantage of both."

It will be seen from the following pages that the author does not side with these critics. He prefers to side with the Pleiades. To his thinking there is a wise way of mixing up religion with *everything*. He is far from being stumbled at seeing RESURGAM at the head of a cemetery, or, IN THE NAME OF GOD, AMEN! at the head of a last will and testament. He is anything but disgusted to find that the name of God appears in some national Magna Charta, that the Gladstones and Bismarcks of the day speak it reverently in Parliament and Reichstag, that legislatures are opened with prayer, that magistrates and even voters are qualified by oaths, that fasts and thanksgivings are proclaimed in state papers, that the legend of a certain Commonwealth is *Qui transtulit sustinet*, that the queen (God bless her!) sends forth her manifestoes with *We Victoria by the grace of God*, that autocrat Nebuchadnezzar in an imperial ukase "talks like a minister" to all his nations and languages. Even the bristling fortress of the Newtonian mathematics seems to him all the better for having in it a little chapel to the Creator; and Te Deums sound not unmusically amid the polyglot of geologic hammers, chemical reagents, and rotating astronomical domes. So he hopes that Newton, Agassiz and Miller will have many successors. It would not much displease him were the time hastily to come when not a scientific lecture is spoken nor a scientific book written which does not in some way pay an emphatic tribute to the Great Author of nature.

The tribute is due. Society needs it more than tongue can tell. Ours are not the ages of faith. An audacious speculation, with its guesses and fictions and insanities, is trying as never before to turn God out of his own world—and with a frightful measure of success. "What France lacks to-day is, not a man, but a God." And Germany is, if possible, worse off still. And both Teuton and Gaul, invited by worse vandals of our own, are freely crossing channel and ocean to lay waste the English-speaking peoples. Many of our strongholds have already fallen into the hands of the invaders. Should all fall it would be "midnight streaked with lightning."

PREFACE.

Not scientific to mix up science and religion in the same book? Then God himself is unscientific, for he has so largely and legibly written himself into that Book of Nature that contains all the sciences that even the heathen "are without excuse for not reading his eternal power and godhead in the things that are made." Is it scientific to attack religion from the side of science, and unscientific to defend it from the same side? Is it scientific to illustrate one science by another, as is daily done without rebuke, and unscientific to illustrate that supreme science which we call religion by that other science which we call astronomy? Is it scientific to notice the gigantic tracks of birds in the rocks of the Connecticut valley, and unscientific to notice in both earthly and heavenly strata the still more gigantic footprints of the Creator? Was it scientific and in excellent taste for the scholar who in the year 1500 found an aged parchment in the monastery of Corwey, in Westphalia, to cry out so that all Europe heard him, "This reads like Tacitus," and unscientific as well as in bad taste for the scholar who finds still more ancient inscriptions in the cloistered heavens, to cry out loudly, "This reads like God"?

LYME, Connecticut.

Contents

I. INSTRUMENTS	7
II. ASPECTS	33
III. ACCURACIES	43
IV. TRANSFORMATIONS	51
V. NUMBERS	99
VI. DISTANCES	109
VII. SIZES	121
VIII. NATURES	127
IX. MOTIONS	139
X. ORBITS	151
XI. PERIODS	161
XII. PERTURBATIONS	171
XIII. SYSTEMS	181
XIV. STABILITIES	193
XV. FORCES	201
XVI. POPULATIONS	213
XVII. MYSTERIES	241
XVIII. MISCELLANIES	271

I. INSTRUMENTS.

1. LIGHT.
2. EYE.
3. TELESCOPE.
4. SPECTROSCOPE.
5. OBSERVATORY.
6. DOCTRINE OF GRAVITY.
7. CALCULUS.

THE GREAT REFLECTING TELESCOPE AT PARIS.

Celestial Empires.

I. INSTRUMENTS.

The wonders of astronomy are shown by means which are wonders in themselves. One of these means is LIGHT. Without this we should know nothing of the heavenly bodies. We cannot touch them, and so know them by the sense of feeling. They send to us no sound, and so we cannot know them by the sense of hearing. Though sometimes called flowers of the sky, and richly deserving the name, they send down to us no fragrance, so that we cannot know them by the sense of smelling. In short, for all our knowledge of them, even of their existence, we are indebted to the sense of sight, and the necessary means of sight is light.

The old Greeks had a divinity whose name was Hermes. He was the messenger of the gods. He was beautiful, was exceeding fleet, carried a wand by which magical things could be done, brought great messages down to men and carried great ones back, was the patron of mysteries as well as of eloquent speech. Light is the modern Hermes. It is the news-carrier from the skies to the earth, and doubtless from the earth to the skies. In beauty, in fleetness, in eloquence, in feats of many names, in bright mysteriousness, it has vastly the advantage of the old messenger; and it has the no small additional advantage of not being light-fingered as well as light-footed, of not being a fiction and a teller of fictions, as was the old Hermes, but, on the contrary, both a glorious fact and a teller of glorious facts.

Who knows what light is? Some suppose it to be a material substance. Still more, just now, suppose it to be vibrations in such a substance. Both are mere suppositions, the latter explaining better than the other certain facts, but leaving other facts unexplained. On all hands light is confessed to be a mystery, and a great one, full of unsolved and apparently unsolvable problems, a great language, of which only here and there a character has come to be understood.

But though a mystery, it has been decomposed into several equal mysteries. Have you seen what one gets by passing light through a prism? What rich and beautiful colors! And they have been found to be the cause of all the beautiful colors in nature and art. In these wide realms what an immense variety of pleasing hues, so grateful to the eye and so useful for distinguishing between objects; nay, what splendor in many flowers and birds and insects and gems and sunset skies! Not even Solomon the Magnificent in all his glory was arrayed like some of these; and both they and Solomon owe all the beauty of their royal and variegated vesture to the variously-colored elements of light. Indeed, without them most of the objects about us would not appear at all, but would hide in the universal dead monotony of white.

It is the light that paints the gold or silver of your hair, the azure or raven of your eye, and the mingled rose and lily of your cheek. The whole landscape about you would be as nothing without light; for it is this that gives the grass its greenness, the water its sparkle, the flower its festival robes, the forest its autumnal array. This work of beautifying man and his surroundings is as much the office of light as it is to show him to his work till the evening. The morning breaks over the eastern hills, and you see to go your way, to build your house, to sow your field, to gather your harvest. Light means both business and beauty.

In what floods is this useful and beautiful element poured forth! With what open-handed freeness does the shining gift come to the cabin as well as to the palace! And where it falls, though it be in Augean stables, it gets no stain from the vileness on which it lingers and which it glorifies. Is this winter? The icicle begins to trickle with dew. The crusted snow, on whose hard surface the feet of walking men a few hours since left no mark, grows soft and yields to an infant's foot. The ground that shows itself here and there, but just now cold and stony to the touch, as you put hand to it again feels warm. What is the matter? It is an open secret. Light is abroad on hard icicle and snowy crust and frozen sod. The soil quickens. The prison of the great chemical forces is thrown open and their chains stricken off. The seeds, the plants, the animals feel a dynamical reinforcing of their life. The currents of health and vigor course through all the veins and arteries of nature with new energy. Take a sun-bath, O invalid! Thin away the trees from your shaded and damp house, O candidate for fevers and agues and malaria of all sorts! Turn over the rough, acid sod, O disconsolate farmer, and let in at the roots of things the *vis medicatrix* of sunshine, and see how soon matters will mend!

Would you have in a twinkling such a faithful picture of yourself or your house or your favorite landscape as a human artist could not make if he would, and perhaps would not make if he could? At a mere trifle of cost would you have all the noted objects in the world, accurately pictured, lying on your parlor-table, or, better still, the faces of dear ones who themselves are gone or going into the invisible? By all means apply to this artist, he does his work so quickly, so cheaply, and so well. It is true that he has his habits which you must humor, his own settled ways of doing things to which you must conform; but when you have done this you will find him a willing and amazing workman, and one that never gets tired.

Do you want to see a traveller that has travelled farther and longer than any other traveller has ever done (I mean this side of the angels, though I am by no means sure that I am bound to make this exception)? You do not need to travel yourself to some distant metropolis, and there, "bored with elbow points through both your sides," catch a glimpse between the shoulders of huzzahing multitudes of some illustrious Humboldt. Just step out into the evening and look up. Here is a ray of light that has just arrived from one of the fixed stars. It has been some millions of years on its way, though it has moved on a straight line and at an unresting pace of more than 180,000 miles a second. Tired? No. Ready to go on other millions of years at the same rate? Yes. What news does this Hermes bring? We shall see. But perhaps he will tell us, among other things, not only that the stars are, but what they are made of, their distances from us and one another, and the measure of their great motions and orbits.

Such is one of our astronomical instruments— a bright, cheery, beautiful, wonderful thing, which has come to be taken as the symbol of almost everything that is exceedingly valuable and splendid—as knowledge and happiness and goodness and even GOD. "God is light, and in him is no darkness at all."

THE EYE is another astronomical instrument. The astronomer needs it in order to use the light. Serviceable as that element is, its service chiefly depends on our being provided with a complex and elaborate instrument that seems made with special reference to it. *We* did not make the eye, we had nothing to do with contriving and adapting its various parts; and yet it is as much an instrument elaborately adjusted to an end as is a watch or a sewing-machine.

This instrument is a very common one, also very uncommon. Every man has a pair of eyes;

every brute animal is at least as well provided for; and some insects have each thousands and thousands of the organs of vision. It would be impossible to put into figures the sum total of those glittering orbs that in the air, on the land, and in the depths of water drink in the rays of light and turn them into vision. But these most common things are at the same time uncommonly wonderful.

Study the human eye as it is shown by anatomists and physiologists, and as we have not space to show it. Behold an organ having reference to an element quite external to itself whose chief source is very distant, and also to millions of objects which compose our scenery of earth and sky; an organ placed in the most elevated part of the body so as to command the most extensive prospect; placed in the front so as to most readily preside over the direction in which we habitually move; placed in a strong, bony socket which defends it from the heavier external injuries; imbedded in a soft cushion, so that its delicate texture cannot be hurt by the bony walls around it as it rests on them and turns swiftly hither and thither at the bidding of the will; furnished with lids to close over it in sleep, to wipe it, to cut off the outer rays of light that would confuse vision, to protect it by their involuntary and instantaneous shutting against the lighter kind of injuries; furnished with an apparatus of muscles by which it can be rapidly turned at choice in any direction so as to vary the field of vision as the needs of life may suggest; furnished with a self-acting system of appliances by which the ball is kept lubricated for easy movement; furnished with a conduit to carry off any superfluous moisture; furnished with just that shape out of ten thousand possible shapes which is the only one that can refract all the rays of light to a single surface, and thus give distinct vision; furnished with a retina, or natural canvas, on which its pictures of external objects can be formed, of just the right size and at just the right distance behind the lenses of the eye; furnished with lenses of different substances having different refractive powers, thereby preventing the light from being resolved into the prismatic colors and thus misrepresenting objects; furnished in front with a perforated membrane that by self-adjustment adapts it to different degrees of light, also with a system of pulleys and ligaments that at a moment's warning alter its convexity and the relative position of parts so as to adapt it to objects at different distances; and, what is most wonderful of all, provided in some mysterious way with the means of expressing the mind itself, so that one may look into its crystal depths and see intellectuality and scorn and wrath and love and almost every spiritual state and action.

Now if this is not an amazing congeries of adaptations there is and can be nothing amazing. If found to be the work of a human artist it would be called a perfect marvel of ingenuity and wisdom. What a source of pleasure, of beauty, of safety, of culture, of business, of power!

And this exquisite instrument is another means of astronomical research, one, it should be noted, altogether inexpensive, in possession of every person, in the use of which we all are practised and skilful, and to whose unaided powers we already owe many valuable astronomical discoveries.

TELESCOPE. This word at once suggests astronomy—as the eye and light do not. All know that it means an instrument for viewing distant objects, and especially the heavenly bodies; and also that by means of it very many striking facts of the far sky, otherwise unattainable, have been reached. They also know that it has the faculty of making some objects seem larger, and of bringing into view objects otherwise invisible.

The original telescope of about three hundred years ago was a very simple affair. It consisted of two curved glasses fastened to a long rod, one to form an image of the object viewed, and the other to magnify that image—called, respectively, the object-glass and the eye-glass.

Gradually improvements came. The glasses were inclosed in a tube so as to cut off the confusing light coming from other objects than the one to be viewed. The imperfect quality and shape of the glass employed gradually, but very slowly, ripened into lenses so pure in quality, so uniform in structure, and so accurately curved, as to leave nothing to be desired in these respects. At first the glass decomposed the light into the prismatic colors, and gave the objects looked at hues that did not belong to them. Means were at length found for correcting this defect. Owing to the difficulty of getting large pieces of pure and even-structured glass, at first the object-glass was very small; but now, though not easily or cheaply. lenses of admirable quality can be made about three feet in diameter. At first it was no small matter to get and steadily hold a telescope in position. So the aid of machinery was invoked, and, finally, the hand of a child is able to point and keep the largest instrument to any quarter of the heavens. Indeed, the tube is made self-moving, so that it will follow a star in its daily path across the sky without any help from the observer. At first there were no contrivances for

THE MERIDIAN CIRCLE, REFRACTING, IN THE PARIS OBSERVARORY.

measuring angles attached to the telescope; now every large instrument is furnished with them in great perfection.

Have you seen a first-class telescope of to-day? It looks almost as complex and mysterious to a beginner in astronomy as do the heavens themselves which it is meant to reveal. And yet it is nothing more than the first telescope of Galileo, supplied with certain devices which have from time to time occurred to astronomers for enabling it to do its work more easily and perfectly. The little one has become a thousand. The rude pole of the great Florentine, with two bits of rounded glass stuck on it, has become a brass palace. I shall not try to describe it by its parts. Anatomy is apt to be destructive. Better take an early opportunity of seeing the wonder; for a wonder it is, of beautiful appearance, of scientific knowledge, and of mechanical skill. It is an elaborate supplemental eye, made out of stone and metal by the crafty and patient hands of three centuries. Here are tons of weight and thousands of parts; but so skilfully framed and balanced is the massive instrument that it turns in every direction almost as noiselessly and easily as do the revolving skies themselves.

This is the largest refracting telescope. The image of the object viewed is formed by refracting the rays of light through a glass of the proper shape. But this image may also be formed by reflection from a mirror or speculum. This may be made much larger than an object-glass, and so can gather much more light. The largest reflecting telescope in the world has a speculum six feet in diameter, a length of fifty-two feet, and a weight of four tons. This instrument, belonging to the Earl of Rosse, at Parsonstown, Ireland, collects 250,000 times as much light from an object as does the naked eye, and so is specially fitted for viewing very faint and distant objects.

With these two sorts of telescopes, the refracting and reflecting, many great results have been obtained — simply by looking. No genius is needed, no long training in the schools, no comprehensive, wide-horizoned learning, no manual or optical skill. Any child, simply by setting eye to the wonderful tube as it points, like some huge columbiad, at the sky, is able to master many illustrious facts which but for it would never have been seen. It is not too much to say that this piece of astronomical ordnance, thundering silently against the nightly skies, has done more execution and brought about more unconditional surrenders than all the artilleries of the nations. It has gained more and greater victories than ever did Alexander or Marlborough or Napoleon; has triumphed oftener and more splendidly than the whole family of Scipios or Cæsars. No blood has stained the azure fields above us; no noise nor smoke has billowed through the concave as our great cylinder has played away on the fortifications of the cloistered heavens; but down, piece by piece, they have come, and science has mounted through the breach and taken wide possession. There remains, it is true, much land to be possessed. Yonder Land of Promise is a very, very wide one; even victors will not overrun it in a hurry. Let us be thankful for so auspicious a beginning. Whether it is more than half the battle remains to be seen.

SPECTROSCOPE. As we have seen, light passed through a prism separates into a band of various colors. This band is called a *spectrum*. If the spectrum is that of an incandescent solid or liquid, its different colors pass into one another without any decided break: if it is that of an incandescent gas or vapor, it is crossed by bright colored lines wholly apart from one another: if it is that of an incandescent solid or liquid shining through an incandescent gas or vapor of lower temperature, then the spectrum is crossed by sharply-defined black lines which vary in place and number according to the nature of the gas—having the same place and number as do the bright lines of the gas where it shines alone. So, when we find the black lines in the spectrum of any star agreeing in these repects with the colored lines peculiar to any gas, it is inferred that this gas is present in an incandescent state in the atmosphere of the star.

But this is not all. It is observed that with increase of density a vapor or gas increases the breadth and number of its bright lines so as to suggest that a continuous spectrum might finally be reached. With an increase of heat the relative intensity of the different lines is sometimes altered; also new lines appear and old ones disappear. If the incandescent substance is moving towards us, its lines are displaced somewhat towards the violet end of the spectrum: if moving away from us, the displacement is towards the red end of the spectrum; and the amount of the displacement is proportioned to the velocity. So when we look at the spectrum of a star we are often able to infer from it, not only what elements enter into its composition, but also the amount and direction of its motion on the line of vision, also something of its state as to temperature and density.

There are difficulties in interpreting many celestial spectra. They are often exceeding faint. And then the very fact that the lines belonging

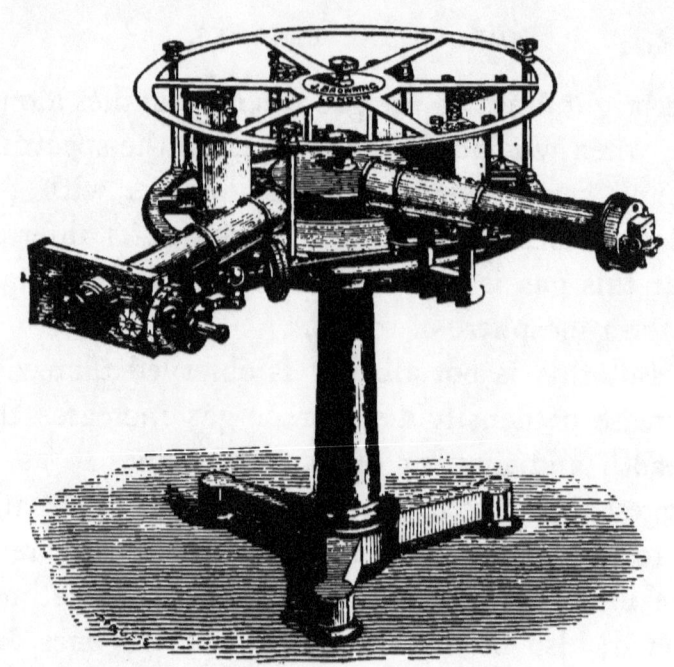

SPECTROSCOPE, WITH RETURNING-BEAM.

TELESPECTROSCOPE.

to any gas or vapor are found to vary with its temperature, density, thickness, motion, distance, as well as with the state of the body behind it in these respects, creates embarrassment. In the more delicate inquiries only experts of special faculty and training can be trusted — and not always they. They sometimes differ widely among themselves. It is still uncertain whether the gaseous envelope of a star may not be so dense and deep and absorbent as to completely cut off the light of a solid nucleus and so report to the eye only its own bright lines. Spectrum analysis is yet in its infancy. But it is a very promising infancy. It has already achieved much, and many other achievements seem to be knocking at the door.

Now the spectroscope is an instrument for making and conveniently examining a spectrum. A compact form of this instrument is attached to the eye-piece of the telescope; and thus connected, by means of the principles just stated, it has made us acquainted with the elementary constitution and present state of many of the heavenly bodies to an extent which a few years ago we could hardly have imagined possible. A great result by means beautifully simple. We look at a little strip of light ribbon, and lo, we know that yonder star has iron and other metals in it—perhaps know that it largely consists of the same sorts of matter we are familiar with in our world. So a new tie is found between us and the far-off regions of the universe; and the instrument that finds it is fitly called *telespectroscope.* At its hands the unity of nature, as looking to one Author, gets a new emphasis.

OBSERVATORY. To use our light and eyes and telescopes to the best advantage we need to be elevated somewhat above the surrounding country. So we get a clearer air. So we get clear of trees and buildings and hills, and command a wide horizon. We need also, especially in these latitudes, shelter for the observer and for his delicate and costly instruments. So we must have a building, and a building so made as to allow our instrument free access to all parts of the heavens. That is, it must have a revolving dome. But a high structure having heavy machinery and instruments to support, and located in a latitude subject to high winds, needs to be very solidly and massively built; especially as every trifling jar in the building is magnified by the whole power of the instrument which it contains. Hence lofty and massive towers have to be built for the higher astronomical purposes. They are so costly that they are generally found in their completed form only in connection with the wealthier universities, or as furnished by endowing cities or nations.

Observatories were in use long before telescopes. As far back as we can trace, lofty and massive structures of many sorts were used for observations on the stars, as the Temple of Belus at Babylon, the tomb of Osmandias in Egypt, to say nothing of pyramids and other high structures in various parts of the world. The earliest modern observatory was built at Cassel in 1561 by the Landgrave of Hesse. In 1576 arose that of Tycho Brahé in the island of Huen. In the next century the royal observatories of Paris and Greenwich were founded. Gradually, as the bearing of astronomical observations on navigation came to be better understood, these watch-towers of the skies and friends of commerce were multiplied, until now every considerable civilized nation has its own observatory—built, equipped, and supported at the public expense. The most noted of these, on account of the magnificence of their appointments or the value of the work they have done or the lustre of the names connected with them, are found at Dorpat, Russia, at Pulkova, Sweden, at Konigsberg and Bonn, Prussia, at Paris, France, at Greenwich, England. To these belong such reputations as those of Arago and Bessel and Struve and Argelander.

In addition to this sort of observatory which has become in our day so sumptuous and beautiful, from whose heights such wide prospects are given, and whose solid and deeply founded strength so seems to defy the rage of the elements and even time itself that it challenges our admiration almost as much as do the sky-conquering instruments it contains, there is another observatory still more remarkable. Are not our common observatories fixtures? Once built, do they not stand on the same spot for ever? If they were only easily transferable from one point of the earth to another, could be cheaply and smoothly spirited away some hundreds of millions of miles nearer the heavenly bodies than they now are, it would sometimes be a great convenience. Well, this is done by means of that underlying observatory that we call the earth. This is the great celestial *lookout*. By its rounded form, transparent atmosphere, and central position among the stars of our firmament (of which more hereafter) it gives us a grand outlook into the populous heavens. By turning on its axis it brings successively into view all parts of the heavens; whereas, without this rotation we could only see a single hemisphere of the sky, except by travelling half round the globe. By its movement about the sun it brings us nearer some of the stars by near two hundred millions of miles than we should be without this motion, and so enables us to discover, as we shall see, important facts otherwise unattainable. And then this travelling observatory of ours moves so smoothly and quietly from place to place that no senses or instruments, however delicate, can detect the slightest tremor. It is so stoutly built, with its endless "munitions of rocks," that we have done our best at describing firmness and stability in a thing when we have likened it to the "foundations of the earth and the everlasting hills." Admirable observatory! ready made to hand—vast in size, sumptuous in appointments beyond any palace we ever saw, usable by everybody without charge and with equal freedom (knock at the door of any other first-class observatory for a like privilege and see what you will get), built and kept in repair without a penny of cost to anybody, carrying us and all our secondary observatories away with magnificent swiftness and comfort on great journeys of discovery and astonishment among the constellations—surely this is a wonderful observatory!

THE CALCULUS AND DOCTRINE OF GRAVITY. There are many arts and sciences which contribute to our knowledge of the heavens. But among these the mathematics are preëminent.

The heavens are mathematically built, and we can advance but a little way towards understanding them before we are obliged to summon to our aid all forms of the science of magnitude. But there is one form of this science, first expounded and used by Newton and Leibnitz about two hundred years ago, which has condensed into itself all the mathematical potentialities, and become the confessed king of all our means of opening up the profounder mysteries of the sky. This is now called the Differential and Integral Calculus. I will not here stop to explain its nature; for this is not necessary to a fair understanding of the great astronomical facts. But for the original discovery of many of these facts a thorough knowledge of this branch of science was indispensable; and no one can now understand the proofs on which a large part of our modern astronomy rests without being profoundly skilled in the use of this great instrument of research. No greater is known to scholars. Taking in his hand the doctrine of gravity and telescopic facts as a glittering two-edged sword, this Black Knight has gone forth among the planets and comets and stars and demanded of them secrets hidden from the foundation of the world—the secrets of their orbits and mutual relations—and has come back heavily laden with spoils richer than ever came from discomfited kings. I cannot say that he is beautiful to look at—as I have said of the light and the eye and the telescope and the observatory. To those not familiar with him he has, I must confess, a forbidding aspect; so far as dress and glitter are concerned, he holds them in supreme contempt; he is no such a holiday warrior as displays himself on parade in peacock millinery of plumes and scarlet and gilt. It is only a plain soldier in battered steel cap and ironsides that we see. But he is a giant; and his sword is sharp as Saladin's and heavy as Richard's; and he is a veteran with an old-time habit of conquering; and, besides, he fights only the battles of truth, progress, and the Lord. Nobody can subsidize him to fight any other. So the hard-favored man of war has much to recommend him. Our militant astronomy would not lose him on any account. It would be losing her right arm. He is a host in himself. And, as his eye is not dim nor his natural force abated with age, but rather the contrary, we may confidently count on still further achievements from this veteran—who is taller than the tallest stone observatory and more commands the secrets of the skies.

Such are some of the instruments of our present astronomy; by no means the whole of them.

Whoever examines the equipment of a first-class observatory will find there many things of which I have said nothing, and of which I propose to say nothing. Indeed, if I should undertake to mention all the astronomical helps, I should be obliged to mention about all the arts and all the sciences, for it would be hard to find a single one which has not contributed in some way and in some degree to our knowledge of the heavens. Especially is astronomy debtor to religion—religion, which is both a science and an art and the common friend and helper of all branches of knowledge, leavening the soul with the nobler sympathies and tastes, purging its sight from gross humors, lifting it to clearer airs and wider horizons, inspiring a sincere love of truth and desire to know God in his works. The great founders of our modern astronomy were religious men. Copernicus, Kepler, and, above all, Sir Isaac Newton, who may be said to have fairly unlocked the heavens to us, were all men to whom science was only the handmaid of devotion, who loved to "think the thoughts of God after him," and to whom the great charm of astronomical study was the fact that "the heavens declare the glory of God and the firmament showeth his handiwork."

Astronomy has many helpers; but the instruments which I have dwelt upon are the chief ones used in helping; and by means of them astronomy has come to great estate. It is to-day a more eloquent oration than orator ever spoke, a loftier epic than ever poet sang, a wealthier harvest than ever turned to gold on the banks of the Nile.

II. ASPECTS.

1. WITH NAKED EYE.
2. WITH TELESCOPE.

II. ASPECTS.

ARISTOTLE, as quoted by Cicero, supposes a people inhabiting the interior of the earth to find their way suddenly for the first time to the surface. What amazement they feel as, with shaded and yet half-blinded eyes, they look towards the magnificent sun and watch the silent majesty of his progress through the heavens! And at the coming on of night, with no less wonder do they look up at the milder glory of the moon, moving westward with what seem millions of bright attendants—Venus with her soft, rich ray, Jupiter with his commanding beam, Mars with his red glance and martial aspect, Vega and Aldebaran and Sirius and Arcturus (where shall one stop?), each with its own peculiar beauty, Pleiades, Hyades, and many another shining group and cluster, till the eye fastens on the astounding arch of the Milky Way with its snowstorm of stars, Cassiopeia, Andromeda, Orion, and all the other superb constellations which garnish the chambers of the north and south, and whose names and fame outdate all history. How the whole heavens seem to sing and exult and *reign* as they sweep westward in their orderly array!

No wonder that astronomy was the earliest of the sciences—that in the morning twilight of the race, on the plateaus and in the transparent airs of Shinar, large-browed men gave themselves up to star-gazing, and asked, "What mean yon radiant objects? Are they not sentinels on the celestial battlements? Are they not guardian spirits keeping watch with eyes aflame over a slumbering world? Are they not worshipful divinities; at least, must not such glorious objects, beaming down on the world so royally, have some controlling influence on its destinies? If they are not gods, do they not nevertheless reign over us *as if* they were?" And not a few bowed their heads and worshipped. Astrologers became cabinet ministers, and nations were governed by horoscopes. But one far wiser than the rest struck his harp and sang, "When I consider the heavens, the work of *Thy* fingers; the moon and the stars which *Thou* hast ordained!"

Such is the aspect of the heavens to the naked eye under ordinary circumstances. But under extraordinary conditions—say a remarkably clear night of January in our latitude; or, better still, the best night in old Chaldæa where the astronomical cradle was rocked; or, still better, the best night in that part of the southern hemisphere on which vertically looks down the brightest page of the whole heavenly book (the zones between 50° and 70°, and where the Milky Way meets the Southern Cross)—a still fairer scene unfolds. Says Humboldt, "The appearance of the Magellanic Clouds, of the brightly-beaming constellation Argo, of the Milky Way between Scorpio, the Centaur, and the Southern Cross, the picturesque beauty, if one may so speak, of the whole expanse of the southern celestial hemisphere, has left on my mind an ineffaceable impression."

Says Sir John Herschel in 1833 from the Cape of Good Hope, "I had already become familiar with most of the great objects of the Southern circumpolar regions so rich in wonders—such as the two Magellanic Clouds, the great nebula about Eta Argus, the great clusters Omega Centauri and 47 Toucani. I may truly say that I felt repaid by the views thus obtained of these most astonishing phenomena for all the trouble and inconvenience of my voyage hither. They are really magnificent, and such as no description can do justice to."

In those Southern latitudes on favorable nights one does not need to be a cultured observer, like Herschel or Humboldt, in order to be impressed with the glory of the celestial scenery. An average pair of eyes with an average manhood behind them will answer, the shining is so jubilant, triumphant. What intense brilliancy! What rejoicing effulgence! What holiday heavens! What conflagrations of glory! Was ever such a dome? Travellers sometimes look up with awe on the pictured and mighty arches that spring airily over St. Peter's. But what a feeble imitation of the great vaulted roof of our Father's house—of the glorious fretted dome that bends over the great cathedral of nature! And yet beneath the Southern Cross multitudes are worshipping fetishes; or, what is worse, not worshipping at all.

This nearly at the sea-level. But what if one gets rid of the lower quarter of the atmosphere by ascending with the astronomer-royal of Scotland the Peak of Teneriffe, some 8,000 feet? Here the usual range of vision is about sextupled, and the grasp of the eye on light is multiplied by thirty-six. "Jupiter shines with extraordinary splendor. The stars hardly seem to twinkle at all. The lustre of the Milky Way and Zodiacal Light is indescribable." Of course still brighter aspects are given at certain still greater elevations where of later years astronomical observations have been made, as at the Etnean Observatory, the highest building in Europe, or at Mounts Whitney or Puno, a matter of some 13,000 feet above the sea.

So appear the heavens to the average naked

eye. But let its pupil be dilated by belladonna and they will appear brighter still. Enlarge that eye till it becomes as large as we sometimes see in men, often in brutes, and always in the ox-eyed Junos of ancient sculpture, and the stars will look into it still more glowingly. Expand that eye again till it matches that orb, "large as a Grecian shield," which Homer ascribes to the Cyclops, or that which terribly rolled in the head of the geologic *deinothere*, and still more glories would add themselves to the already blazing heavens. Once more expand till the eye-diameter is that of the speculum of the largest reflecting telescope, which gathers from a star 250,000 times as much light as the average eye receives, and every celestial object will be brightened a quarter of a million of times.

Now this is the eye which the user of such a telescope practically has. A star as it appears to the naked eye is a tame and dull thing compared with the same object as it shows in the field of a great telescope. Sir William Herschel seldom looked at the larger stars in his great reflector, because their blaze was injurious to his sight. He says, "The first appearance of Sirius announced itself at a great distance like the dawn of the morning, and came on by degrees, increasing in brightness till this brilliant star at last entered the field of the telescope with all the splendor of the rising sun, and forced me to take my eye from the beautiful sight." In the Rossian reflector one could almost imagine Sirius to be a divine face or shield. And the Pleiades are no longer *the Seven Stars* that one has so long known and admired, but that group transfigured almost beyond recognition. The great cluster in the constellation called Hercules, or in the Centaur, seems to have had a door opened in heaven just behind it, and to be swimming in the unspeakable glory that pours forth. And various colors appear where the naked eye hardly saw more than one. Some stars are red, some blue, some green, some yellow, some white; in short, all the colors of the rainbow or of the gems that sparkle in the cabinets of kings are represented. Of course, if the great telescopic eye that peers up from its low place through the thick skies of Ireland could be set up on the summit of the Californian Mount Hamilton, we should see still greater things than these. Would not one be reminded of the city whose foundations are garnished with all manner of precious stones? and would he not seem to catch glimpses of the amethyst and the emerald and the jasper and the ruby and the beryl, and still other jewels that make up the twelve foundations of the city of God?

It were worth our while to use a telescope were it only for the new beauty which it gives the heavens. And it also gives us a *truer* view of them, as well as one more magnificent. Our photographs as well as our painted portraits often flatter us. Somehow we have been made out better-looking than we are. We have been brightened up far beyond our "happiest expression." But it is impossible to brighten up the pictures of the heavenly bodies till they seem more glorious than they actually are. Our largest instruments bring to us only a small part of their real brightness. In fact they are like their Maker in this respect. We cannot get too bright a conception of him. When we have done our best to make it fair and grand, we know that we have fallen infinitely short of doing him justice. Do not be afraid, O painter of the Infinite; give wings to your imagination, summon all your powers of expression, use your fairest colors, glorify your canvas, get as near as you can to a perfect ideal of mingled loveliness and majesty; in a word, invoke all the cunning of thought and hand that the greatest masters have had, what is that picture of yours, after all, but an image dimmed by innumerable reflections of the Infinite!

III. ACCURACIES.

1. OF OBSERVATION.
2. OF THEORY.

III. ACCURACIES.

In the earliest time men contented themselves with such facts about the heavenly bodies as a mere gazing at them might discover. But, at least as early as the time of the Greek astronomer Hipparchus (B. C. 125), it became clear that in order to see whether any changes are going on in the sky, and, if so, what changes and how great, it would be necessary to *locate* the stars carefully, that is, give their position in the sky with reference to two fixed circles that cut each other at right angles, just as we now give the situation of places on the earth by their latitudes and longitudes. Accordingly Hipparchus, and after him Ptolemy, prepared instruments for measuring angles and made catalogues of many stars, giving their distance from the equinoctial and from its intersection with the ecliptic as accurately as their instruments would allow. But these instruments were so rude that they could not measure accurately a smaller arc of the sky than ten minutes—about one-third of the moon's apparent diameter. But Tycho Brahé, a Danish astronomer, who died A. D. 1681, was not satisfied with such astronomy as this, and finally succeeded in so improving the old instruments as to measure an arc of ten seconds—a measure sixty times more delicate and refined than the other. But now, by means of the telescope and its various appointments, we are able to measure the hundredth part of a second, that is, about the 180,000th part of the moon's apparent diameter. We have, therefore, reached an accuracy a thousand-fold greater than Tycho was able to secure. Such a refinement of observation would have been incredible to astronomers of a few generations back. It is now almost incomprehensible to those who have not particularly studied the present ways and means of securing such accuracy. And yet, like many other mysterious things, it is a fact. Argelander, a German astronomer, has made a catalogue of 324,000 stars whose places are given somewhat after this supreme style of accuracy. But even this can be exceeded under special circumstances. When the very utmost of delicate measurement is required, as in determining the distance of the sun, we can by certain expedients manage to tenfold that last astonishing accuracy and measure the 1,000th part of a second—the 2,000,000th part of the moon's diameter on the sky. Nay, you will find that in measurements for finding some stellar distances astronomers even take account of such extremely small things

ACCURACIES.

as the 10,000th part of a second—a space about equal to the apparent breadth of a human hair at the distance of 94 miles from the observer. Such achievements are chiefly due to the telescope. It is to angles what the microscope, enabling us to count 112,000 lines in an inch, is to linear dimensions.

After this wonderful manner astronomers measure space. They deal with time in very much the same way. If you go to some observatory, the experienced observer whom you will find there tells you that he can with ease, while observing, mentally divide a second of time into ten equal parts. If you look into a scientific journal you will, perhaps, find the times of the beginning and ending of the next solar eclipse at a given place given to the tenth of a second. If you look into some astronomical text-books you will find it stated that the interval between two consecutive returns of a star to the same meridian has demonstrably not altered by one hundredth of a second for the last 2,000 years, will be almost sure to find the interval between two consecutive returns of the sun to the same tropic expressed in figures that take account of the 10,000th part of a second, and perhaps will read that this interval has shortened by 595,000ths of a second in 100 years.

Such extreme accuracy would be of no use in

surveying a field. The millionth part of a square inch of ground, even in a city, is "nothing to nobody." But in astronomy, on account of the immensity of its spaces, the very small mistake of one second in locating an object may alter our estimate of its distance from us by 200,000 times the evidently great distance of the sun. Also these extremely delicate measurements enable us to answer satisfactorily such questions as these: Are the fixed stars really *fixed?* Are any of them physically connected with one another in systems somewhat like the solar system? Does the law of gravity prevail among them? What are their orbits, periods, distances, and sizes? Are they stationary in respect to us? Is our solar system itself in motion among the stars? And if so, towards what part of the heavens is our course directed, at what rate, and around what centre, if our path is an orbit? Were it not for the fact that our instruments enable us to take account of changes in the sky that are almost nothings, such questions could never have been answered. What great questions they are! No better illustration, perhaps, out of the moral field could be given of the importance of littles. We are told that the happiness of individuals and families depends upon them. We have seen vast boulders pivoted on mere points of rock, and the fortunes of individuals, families, and even empires rising or sinking in the balance by the weight of a mere grain of circumstance. A glorious character may be gradually built up, like coral islands, by means of daily acts that in themselves are merest mites, too inconsiderable to attract notice. And so the glory of our modern astronomy is largely conditioned on measurements so small as to be almost incredible, and quite incomprehensible to people at large.

But the accuracy of *observation* is not the only astronomical accuracy that is marvellous. By means of the law of gravity as interpreted and applied by that great instrument of investigation, the Calculus, the astronomer can sit in his study, and without looking out of his window, calculate just where in the sky one may find many seemingly very erratic bodies at any given remote time. Where will those strangely zig-zagging bodies called planets be ten years hence? At what times, backward or forward indefinitely, are eclipses of the sun or moon to be found? Can you tell other generations when and where to look for another occultation of yonder star, another transit of Venus, another return of yonder comet that has not appeared before within the whole time of astronomic records? Such questions as these, discouraging as they look at first view, can now be answered with astonishing precision. Some of the most useful examples of such precision are embodied in the Nautical Almanac—a book published annually for use in navigation. This gives for years in advance the apparent distances, say at Greenwich, of the moon from the sun and from certain fixed stars for every three hours—gives them so as never to involve an error of more than five seconds of a degree. This though in order to do so it is necessary to take account of twenty-eight disturbances in the motion of the moon. By taking account of some thirty disturbances more—if he has time enough to do it, and patience enough, and, I should add, enough indifference to misspent toil and genius and mathematics — the astronomer may reduce this trifling possible error to a mere ghost of its former ghostly self. But what would be the use! Such exactness would be thrown away on the problem of the longitude. The sailor can know his place on the seas sufficiently well without it. All that a *lunar* can do to secure property and life is done already. And yet we are not to despise that extreme possible theoretical exactness. It has no small educational value, and may turn to great account in equipping astronomy for brilliant victories in the near future.

IV. TRANSFORMATIONS.

1. EARTH.
2. MOON.
3. SUN.
4. PLANETS.
5. COMETS.
6. METEORS.

IV. TRANSFORMATIONS.

UNDER the various astronomical instrumenst certain old astronomical friends appear with surprisingly new faces. They may even be said to be *transformed*. They are the Earth, the Moon, the Sun, and five planets, viz., Mercury, Venus, Mars, Jupiter, and Saturn. Perhaps I should add comets and meteors.

All these have been familiarly known, the chief of them under their own proper names, time out of mind. And, notwithstanding the stories that have at times got abroad to the prejudice of two or three of them, they have always maintained the most friendly relations with one another and with mankind. They have never met in the shock of set battle, never collided, never even fallen out by the way in some transient unpleasantness. So far as we know, here is a community without a quarrel, a family without a family jar. For now untold ages this family has held together in unbroken harmony. It is true that we sometimes speak of "*disturbances*" among them—say that they disturb one another's motions. But we do not mean by this any unfriendly interaction; only such as may obtain, and always does obtain, between the members of the most exemplary and loving of households. Do not such members influence one another? Is not the career of each more or less modified by that of every other? Instead of mutually injuring they are mutually helpful. As much, doubtless, is true of our celestial household. What have been called "*disturbances*" are merely the friendly interactions and agitations that go to make a healthy and balanced system. And, as far as man is concerned, the poorest in repute of all that shining group has always a balance to his credit at the Bank of Humanity, does somewhat to brighten our homes, decorate our sky, expand our minds, and lift our thoughts towards the Creator. And together they have furnished the stepping-stones to most of our ulterior astronomy. We never could have known the distances, sizes, motions, forces in other parts of the heavens save by means of what we have learned from these friendly contributors. They have contributed to our mathematics and instruments of observation the discipline and culture and facts without which we must have halted at the very threshold of the sky. They have furnished the units of comparison, the measuring-rod, by which the angel of science has measured the descending celestial city of the astronomical heavens.

THE EARTH from whose dust men were first made, on whose surface they have always lived, and from whose bosom they have always drawn their support, has a clear right to be considered our friend. Some think it deserves to be called our mother—"Mother Earth."

And yet this friend, though well known, was also very poorly known till of late. It was not thought to be a heavenly body at all. By far the greater part of its surface was wholly unexplored. It was supposed to have neither rotation nor revolution. Its shape and size and relations to the other heavenly bodies were grossly misconceived even by the most intelligent; while to people at large in the most advanced communities it was only a great plain resting on—they knew not what. A few hundred miles from their capitals exhausted the geography of the ancient Assyrians, Babylonians, Phœnicians, and Egyptians. The best informed of the Greeks and Romans knew scarcly anything of other countries than those just about the Mediterranean. The greater part of Asia and Africa, the whole of America, and the ocean islands were unknown to the rest of the world till about 400 years ago. And what was considered to be known was known after a very scanty fashion. A map of the earth as it was known to Copernicus and Galileo would not tax very much the memory of our children.

Since then great advances have been made. The old friend has put on quite a new face. We find it to be a heavenly body. Instead of being an indefinite plain resting on something else, if not on a monster elephant and tortoise, it is now known to be a round body some thousands of miles in diameter, lying out entirely unsupported in space, practical vacancy on all sides of it—in short, as the Scripture says, "hung on nothing."

Latterly the surface of this great globe of which the ancients knew so little has been greatly revealed. And when the matter is inquired into we find that the revelation is largely due to the telescope and its adjuncts. Indeed, this instrument has given us all our accurate geography. We have now determined astronomically and with great exactness the latitude and longitude of all the more important points of the earth; have also, by the same means and by dredging, gotten a general idea of the great ocean-bed. Every civilized nation has provided charts of its own coasts so accurately made that they represent the contour of the land and of the neighboring sea-bottom with almost the fidelity of a Dutch portrait or of a photograph. This has been done in connection with a system of triangulation in which the telescope and its helpers play a conspicuous part. Some of us have in our libraries the Coast Survey Charts of the United States, and some of us have remembered, as we admired them, that without astronomical instruments and learning we should never have had these beautiful and minutely accurate delineations of that astronomical body on which we live.

The telescope is also the condition of all extensive ocean-voyaging. The coast surveys provide for the safety of navigation along certain favored shores; but if we are to have that knowledge of the wide earth that comes from immense commerce and travel, means must be furnished for passing over the oceans freely and safely in every direction. In order to do this the sailor must be able to find his exact place on the deep at any moment. Is he near a lee shore? Have not the strong winds or crafty currents beneath been setting him out of his course and near rocks? And it is not enough for him to consult his dead-reckoning and chronometer; he must verify them by observing certain heavenly bodies, and by consulting that famous Nautical Almanac which is in some sort the sailor's bible, doing for him on the natural deeps what the Bible offers to do on the spiritual. The substructions of the Nautical Almanac are the Greenwich Observatory, the telescope, and the doctrine of gravity. These are what we come to if we dig down to the very bottom of things and ask how that indispensable *vade mecum* was made. Just as, if we dig through the crust of the earth at any point, we come to the one crystalline rock that underlies the whole, so, if we dig through the Nautical Almanac at any page, we find astronomy at the bottom. This which has made the deep comparatively safe, and has gradually covered it with inquisitive traffickers and travellers into all lands, has been the means of a vast accession to our knowledge of the earth. What crowded maps and bulky geographies are now on the tables of our scholars, and even on the desks of the common school! A thoughtful man sees a telescope in the background and between the lines of every one of them. Compare them with the maps and geographies of three centuries ago, and what a difference!

The chemistry of the stars is properly counted a part of astronomy. So terrestrial chemistry and geology and other natural sciences, which within the present century have added so much to our knowledge of our globe, have really an astronomical character, not merely because the earth is a heavenly body, but because of the aid which the study of the other heavenly bodies has given in developing them. The geologist goes to his work in distant countries in ships astronomically steered, studies the intimate structure and succession of fossils and rocks with optical glasses perfected chiefly for astronomical uses, interprets the past of the earth in view of climatic conditions growing out of astronomical relations, and perhaps concludes with Humboldt that "our knowledge of the primeval ages of the world's physical history does not extend sufficiently far to allow our depicting the present condition of things as one of development." The chemist uses in his work light and heat and other agents whose chief reservoir is found in the astronomical field proper, and to the understanding of which the study of astronomy has furnished a chief incentive; and he daily gives thanks, or ought to, for the spectroscope which so splendidly helps his galvanic battery in detecting the composition of bodies. So of our botany, zoology, and other natural sciences. They are all debtors, and some of them heavily so, to astronomy.

The telescope has also helped us to all our precise knowledge of the shape and size of the earth. Its general roundness is known by other means; but we have to use the telescope with its appliances in order to know that we do not live on a perfect sphere (of course on so large a body we make no account of even our highest mountains), but on a sphere somewhat flattened on opposite sides, and also to know what are the exact values of the longest and shortest diameters. This knowledge is gained by measuring arcs of the meridian with very great care in all parts of the world, and telescopes have been indispensable to such measurements. By these it has been found that our extremes of diameter differ by about 26 miles, while our mean diameter is 7,912 miles.

This great almost globe—so our astronomy of the last few centuries has been teaching us, in defiance of the general belief of mankind from the beginning—turns quietly on itself once in twenty-four hours, without the least noise or jar, and with a perfectly uniform motion, thus making the whole heavens with their contents seem to revolve about us daily. In addition we have learned that our rotating earth moves about the sun in about 365 days, with no appreciable change in this period from age to age. Although we do not perceive either of these motions by the sense of hearing or feeling, so smoothly and noiselessly are they made, yet they both are sufficiently proved to us by the fact that they furnish the simplest and a perfect explanation of the great daily and yearly motions in the sky.

THE MOON. Another old friend, as old as the

THE MOON, FULL AND HALF-FULL.

earth or older. Ever since man was it has been showing its broad, hearty, good-humored face in the sky, none the less cheery from being considerably freckled. Who can doubt its friendliness! especially since its friendly looks are so supported by friendly deeds. What a relief to the night! What an illuminator of stumbling paths! What a soft and delicious bath of silver it makes for land and sea! How the sea swells lovingly towards it and tries to follow it all round the globe, as if it could not bear to lose sight of it, and grows pure and vital by the effort! What meant the old-time prophet when he said, "Blessed of the Lord be his land for the precious things brought forth by the sun, and for the precious things put forth by the moon"? Beautiful, friendly, smiling Moon! True, some say that thy smile is false and treacherous, that thou smitest when thou smilest. So said the ancient Egyptians. So said the astrologers of the Middle Ages and later, especially when they saw the Moon in conjunction with Saturn. Then nothing was too bad for it to do. Then let men look out for colds, convulsions, jaundice, epilepsy—"all the ills that flesh is heir to." Woe to him that was born under the "House of the Moon." And the bad stories still linger. Bad to sleep in the moonlight, is it? Hurts certain crops, does it? That is slander—

shall I say superstition? We will believe neither the ancients nor the moderns against our old friend. When was there a friend, especially a fair one, and never a word spoken against her? She does not, Judas-like, betray with a kiss. Let the poets go on praising the queen of the night as with far-flowing, spangled robes she moves majestically across the heavens. Even let them, if they will, call her a goddess, the "goddess of the silver bow," Diana, Artemis, Phœbe, Proserpina, Hecate, Astarte; only let them not worship her, as men once did, and as even Solomon the Wise seems to have done.

> "With these in troops
> Came Ashtaroth, whom the Phœnicians called
> Astarte, queen of heaven, with crescent horns;
> To whose bright image nightly by the moon
> Sidonian virgins paid their vows and songs;
> In Sion also not unsung, where stood
> Her temple on the offensive mountain, built
> By that uxorious king whose heart, though large,
> Beguiled by fair idolatresses, fell
> To idols foul."

That was indeed to be "moon-struck," "lunatic."

What men knew about the Moon till lately was what they could learn by the naked eye only. The common use of the eye shows a luminous disk about half a degree in diameter, variously shaded, apparently moving westward with all the other bright objects in the sky, and at the same time creeping eastward among them so as to make a complete circuit of the sky in about twenty-seven days—in nearly the same period waning from a full disk to nothing and then waxing back to the old fulness, in addition suffering occasional eclipses which, after eighteen years, repeat themselves in the same order and at the same intervals as before. This period was called *Saros*.

These facts are easily noticed, and have been familiar to men from time immemorial. But careful observation, long watching, trained eyes, and most of all, a just theory and fine instruments, especially the telescope, have by degrees, but more especially within the last few years, added so much to our knowledge of the Moon that "the former things shall not be remembered nor come into mind." Let us notice some of the chief points of interest that have been discovered.

Its light is not its own, but is the reflected light of the sun. If it were self-luminous it would, of course, always appear at the full. But it is not seen at all when the sun cannot shine on the face that is turned towards us. When the sun comes to hold such a place that it can begin to shine on that side it begins to appear luminous, and gradually the luminous surface enlarges as the position of the sun becomes more and more favorable, until at last we have the full moon. Also, the spectroscope, which has found that each self-luminous body has its own peculiarity of light, finds that the light which comes to us from the moon is that of the sun. So the glory of the moon is a borrowed one. She is a great reflector. She borrows, but always forgets to return the most of what she borrows. In fact she returns only a very trifling percentage of it. But, like many other people, she is very liberal with what does not belong to her. She scatters it freely right and left. We get from her at the full thousands of times as much light as we get from all the stars together. But we pay her back "in her own coin" even more liberally—principal with twelve hundred per cent. interest. A part of this is the very light she sends to us—as we may see in the faint illumination of the moon's first quarter when the "old moon appears in the arms of the new." But most of the light we send comes to us directly from the sun. We also pay with what we have borrowed. So we cannot cast stones at our neighbor.

The shape of the moon is globular, like that of the earth. At the full it seems like a silver plate. Then it looks as if being eaten up by little and little of some invisible monster. We seem to see the ragged edge and the marks of his teeth! At last all is gone. Only, however, to come again in a new crescent, and slowly wax to its former roundness. Notwithstanding this apparent variety of shapes or "phases"—crescent, half-circle, gibbous, full-circle—the moon really has but one shape, and that is such as the earth has, viz., that of a globe. Only a round body could show the "phases." And as we look at the face through a telescope, we notice that the central parts have that distincter look that belongs to the central parts of a rounded surface.

The telescope practically takes us very near the moon, and, especially with the help of photography, enables us to make a map of it in some respects better than any map of the earth can be. Behold a tremendous Switzerland with vast chasms, walled plains, lofty mountains, enormous craters of what seem extinct volcanoes! It is as if some madcap ocean, at the supreme moment of one of its wildest moods, had been suddenly stiffened into stone. What wild and savage grandeur of disorder, as if from some ancient battle and carnival of Titans and demons, as if from the Miltonic battle between the faithful and unfaithful angels!

> "From their foundations loos'ning to and fro
> They pluck'd the sealéd hills with all their load,
> Rocks, waters, woods, and by the shaggy tops
> Uplifting, bore them in their hands . . . . .

> Main promontories flung, which in the air
> Came shadowing, and oppressed whole legions armed.
> So hills amid the air encountered hills,
> Hurled to and fro in jaculation dire."

As we gaze, we feel face to face with another, though immensely rougher, earth. We see mountains worthy of such proper names as Tycho, Copernicus, Newton. We see great chasms and craters, with ragged, precipitous sides; such as volcanoes and earthquakes sometimes make in our ground. We see sunrises and sunsets among the hills—shadows of peaks and of mountain ranges that creep along lunar valleys, as the elevation of the sun varies, just as we see them creep along our terrestrial ones. We see at once that the height of many of these peaks, and the breadth of many of these craters and crevasses, are enormous when expressed in terms of the moon's apparent diameter; and as soon as we learn the real distance and size of the moon we can find that thirty-nine of the peaks are higher than Mont Blanc, and several of the craters more than fifty miles across, while one crater is more than twice that. What moonquakes there must have been in some far back time, in comparison with which the earthquakes that broke up and tossed about our strata and piled our Alps and Andes were mere child's play!

While thus we notice an earth-surface we also

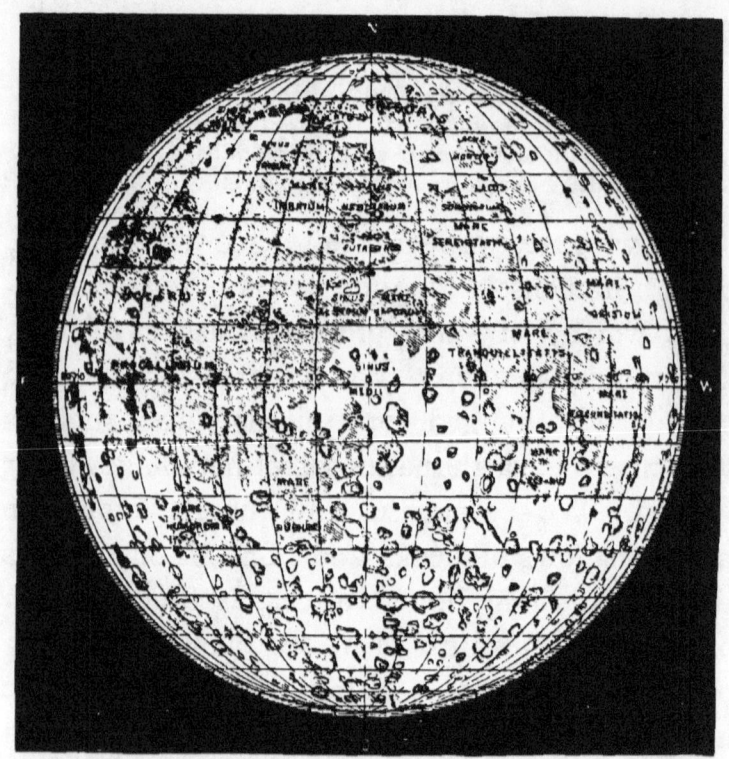

MAP OF THE MOON'S HEMISPHERE.

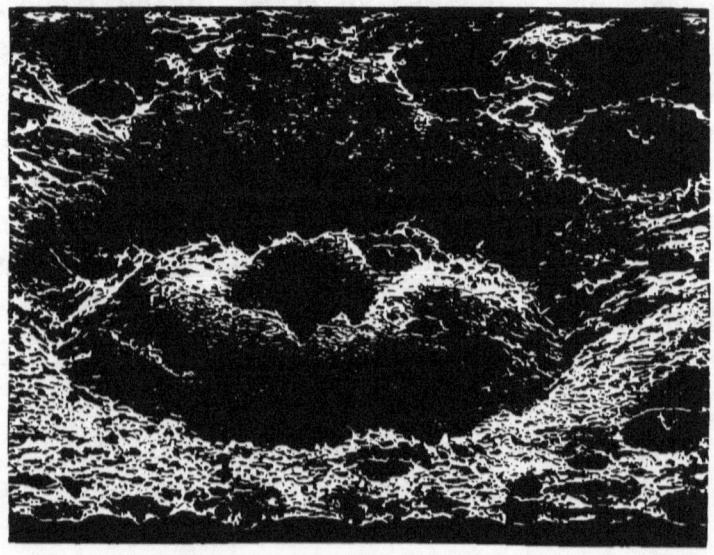

A LUNAR MOUNTAIN.

notice the absence of some things that belong to our earth. We see no signs of water, though we see what look like ancient sea-beds, and though, when our instruments were rude and our thoughts ruder, we thought we saw in the Moon's spots the waters themselves, and gave them names accordingly—as the Sea of Plenty, Lake of Dreams, Sea of Serenity, Lake of Death, Ocean of Tempests. No clouds have been detected, nor, indeed, any signs of an atmosphere to support them. How this is to be reconciled with other appearances just mentioned is still an unsolved problem. Have the ancient waters retired beneath the surface? Have they gone into chemical unions and solids? Has the great Creator restored to nothing that which from nothing he took? Or are those seeming ancient sea-beds mere seemings? As yet we cannot answer.

Of course we are compelled to say that no beings constituted *like men* can exist in a world that has neither air nor water. But that is not saying that the Moon has no inhabitants. Surely an infinite Being could produce living creatures that do not require to breathe and drink; and the extremely different conditions under which animal life flourishes on the earth are very suggestive of the possibility of still wider ranges.

The Moon never shows us but one face. From

year to year we see the same objects on its surface, saving on a little of the margin.

This is what has hitherto been done in the way of perusing with our telescopes the features of the Moon—not all, however, that has been *claimed* to be done. Some German astronomers at one time thought that they had caught glimpses of a town, of a fortress, of canals, and even of green pastures. But this is now more than discredited; it is ridiculed almost as freely as what is known as the "lunar hoax." When Sir John Herschel went to the Cape of Good Hope many years ago for astronomical purposes, there appeared in the journals what purported to be a letter from him giving account of certain great discoveries made by his new refractor from that favorable standpoint. "He had discovered on the surface of the Moon, in addition to many larger objects, herds of winged men with ape-faces, and even shells and flowers." The story got large credence for a time—a very brief one—with the unscientific public, and then burst, as so many other bubbles called scientific have done and are likely to do. An unscrupulous wag had tested the credulity of mankind and found it to be immense.

THE SUN. A friend also. Does it not give us day and light us to our various employments and enjoyments? Does it not paint the landscape with all the glory of colors—greening the grass, flushing the rose, besnowing the lily? Does it not quicken the dull ground into fruits and grains and forests and flowers? Does it not stir the air into breezes to fan our fevered brows, equalize temperatures, fill the sails of commerce, work stagnation into purity? Is it not the indispensable condition of all our physical comfort and even of all vegetable and animal life? Without it the earth would be a benighted desert, a depopulated iceberg. Age after age (for who shall say how many thousand years?) the old Sun has been gloriously shining away at such goodly and friendly work, like the greater Sun who made it, never pausing a moment in its silent beneficence, however provokingly treated, and visiting all nations and generations with the same impartial beam. And so all men have been wont to look upon and welcome it in its steadfast daily visits as a steadfast friend, some even as a benevolent divinity.

Among the latter one may almost class some scientists. Hear one of them. "The Sun is the life of the earth. It is the common origin, the inexhaustible source whence have been derived for millions of centuries past all terrestrial powers, all mechanical and physical energy, as well as the *powers of all living creatures*, both vegetables and animals. The solar heat is the final source of the force manifested by society." This is talking like a pagan and sun-worshipper. As one listens he would think the Sun to be the creator and builder as well as governor of the world, instead of being the very serviceable brute friend which the Great Friend has set to work in our behalf and which our bodies could not well get along without. Far from us be such science. We call the Sun a warm friend and a very great one; but by such pictorial language we mean nothing more than that it is the indispensable instrument of vast comforts and blessings to us. So much is true.

This notwithstanding some drawbacks. Let men not venture to turn naked eye on its glory: why should they be made blind, as some careless astronomers have been? Do not with bare brow defy the summer noon: why shouldst thou fall by a sunstroke or rave with a fevered brain? Parchings and scorchings and droughts, brazen skies and barren soils, are they not the occasional troubles that we fear and deplore and pray against? Yes, certainly there are drawbacks to this fervid, hot-headed friend of ours. But where are the friends without dangerous points and drawbacks? All our friends have a dangerous side to them— dangerous in proportion to their greatness and

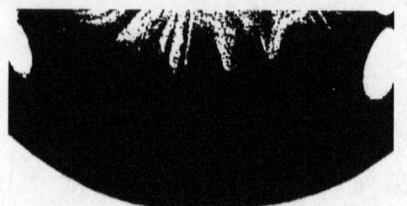

SOLAR CORONA, IN 1857 AND 1871.

power. *Royal* friends need to be dealt with after a manner of special carefulness. We must not abuse them, we must not trifle with them, else their harming will be as vast as their helping has been.

A circular disk of insufferable splendor, having two apparent motions, like those of the Moon (one in common with all the stars and the other among the stars), and sometimes eclipsed partly or wholly by the Moon coming between us and it, this is about all the naked eye discovers or the ancients knew about the Sun. They had their conjectures. Some thought so splendid an object must be a leading divinity. They called him Helios or Apollo or Baal or Osiris, and worshipped him as the brother of the Moon. And those of wiser views *knew* absolutely nothing of the real form and nature of the great luminary which the vulgar adored. Anaxagoras guessed that it is a mass of incandescent matter, and but for the eloquence of his friend Pericles would have lost his life for his boldness. As it was, he lost only his country; no great loss, considering what an unreasonable country it was.

So it was till quite modern times. As soon as the telescope was invented, what had been thought a surface of uniform brightness was seen to be far otherwise. The whole face appeared mottled—

first by spots of special brightness now called *faculæ*, secondly by spots of special darkness. The latter are what are commonly called Sun-spots. Like the bright spots, they have every variety of form, and show on their margin a penumbra. When a telescope of still higher power is brought to bear on the face, it appears covered with pores or points less bright than the intervening spaces. In the immediate neighborhood of the dark spots the better glasses show a still more striking aspect—multitudes of bright spots tending to a linear arrangement.

In a photograph of the Sun the central parts appear in relief, the margin relatively dim and foreshortened. It is plainly a *globe* whose picture we see—a globe some of whose parts are nearer to us by its whole semi-diameter than others.

A little watching of this globe with a telescope shows that it is revolving on an axis. The dark spots and faculæ are plainly in motion in a common direction, and some of them maintain substantial identity for months. The motion of these is equable, from west to east, and completes a circuit in from twenty-five to twenty-eight days. It is most naturally accounted for by supposing that the Sun, like the Earth and the Moon, revolves on itself.

Unlike the Earth and the Moon, it is a self-

TRANSFORMATIONS. 71

luminous globe. In all circumstances, when our atmosphere is without clouds, the Sun shows a full orb when above the horizon. Besides we know of no other luminous object to furnish the light by which it shines. Also, as before stated, reflected light has a different optical property from that which is original with the body from which it last comes, and this test applied to the Sun shows that it is self-luminous.

It is but a step farther to the fact that this self-luminous globe is a globe *on fire*, and on fire after a most terrible fashion. We might guess as much from the heat it sends to us from so great a distance as it plainly is. But our spectroscopes put the matter beyond doubt. They find that the Sun gives the spectrum of a burning body. How great its heat must be can be inferred from the intensity of its light and heat at the surface of the Earth. The most vivid flames we can make appear almost as so much blackness when interposed between us and the Sun. As to its heat, what it is at the equator on some sultry summer noon we know; and we know also that after leaving the Earth's atmosphere in going towards the Sun the heat directly radiated from it must increase as the square of the Sun's distance from us diminishes. But inasmuch as a very great change in the place of an observer on the earth makes no easily appreciable change in the place of the Sun in the sky we know that its distance from us must be very great, and, consequently, that the heat at its surface must be incomprehensibly enormous—some say four million degrees Fahrenheit, and all should say enough to turn the most refractory substances known to us into gases or vapors instantly, or to convert a globe of ice as large as the earth into steam in a few minutes; in short, thousands of times greater than any furnace ever sent forth, greater than the very lightning itself can furnish, whose flash across the Sun's face is obscuring.

It is only a step farther to say that the Sun is a globe completely covered with a fiery ocean. Whether the globe is throughout liquid or gaseous and vaporous is still a matter of dispute; but that the surface consists of mobile matter, incandescent, and in a state of intense agitation, and sometimes of terrible storm, is admitted by all astronomers. The faculæ and dark spots for the most part are incessantly changing in form and place, and sometimes a spot flies to pieces almost as a cake of ice does when cast on a rock. Under favorable conditions we can see at the edge of the disk a colored stratum with protuberances, giving mainly the spectrum of hydrogen, the protuberances often becoming immense scarlet jets—

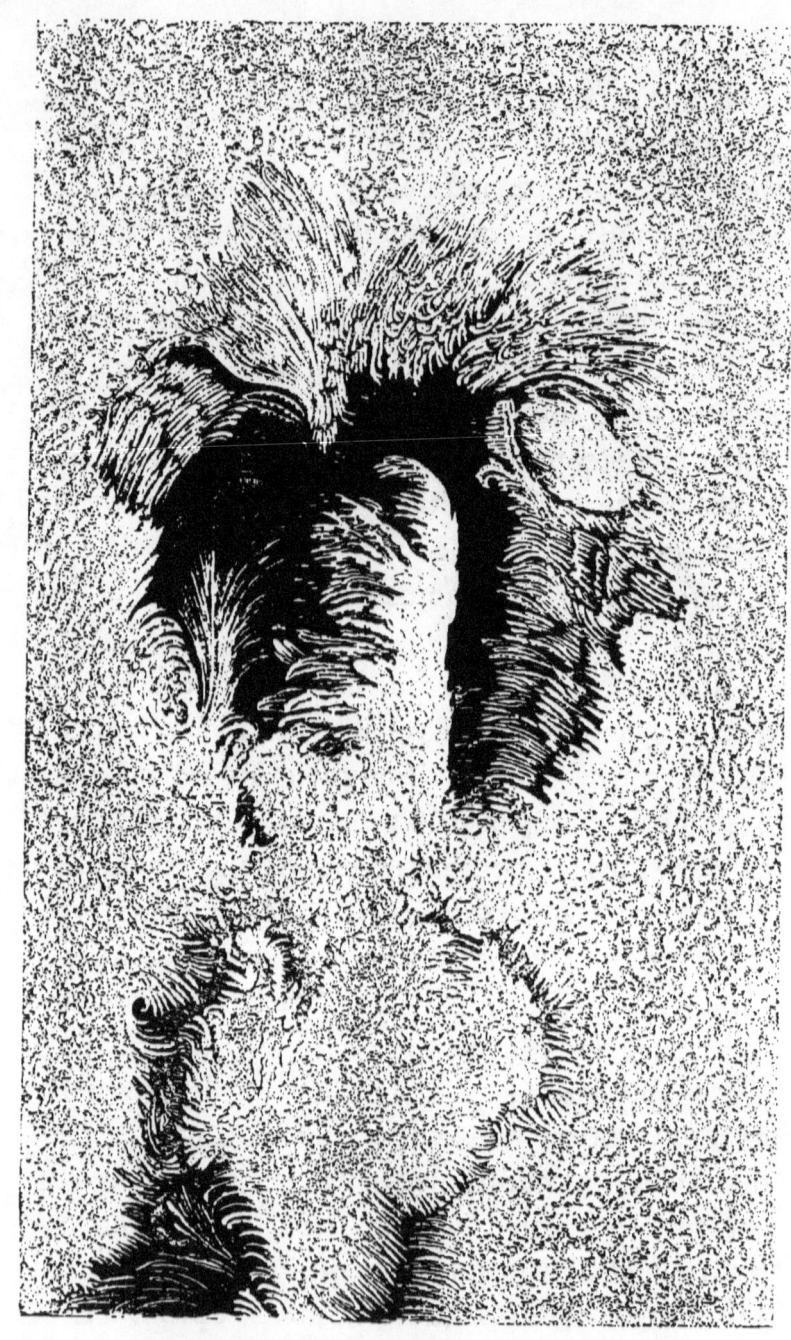

THE SOLAR PHOTOSPHERE: SUN-SPOTS.

sun-geysers; sometimes entirely detached from the body of the Sun, and sometimes rising above it more than one-third its whole apparent diameter, which will be seen to mean a matter of 300,000 miles. Such facts, taken in connection with the vast heat of the Sun and the vast chemical actions necessarily going on amid its tremendous fires, warrant us in saying that never was earthly ocean or atmosphere so tossed into madness as is that solar ocean on which our eyes refuse to linger.

The scarlet atmosphere of hydrogen is surrounded by still another atmosphere of far lighter and as yet unknown material, best seen in a total eclipse of the Sun. This is called the *corona*. The underlying colored region is called the *chromosphere*, while the disk as commonly seen is known as the *photosphere*. When the rays from the more effulgent photosphere are cut off by the moon the more attenuated and cooler envelopes become visible. Then for a few moments they become objects of intense study to astronomers— as yet not altogether satisfactory study so far as the corona is concerned. Its widely different aspects and conditions at different times embarrass both telescope and spectroscope. One might reasonably expect a large variety in these respects in an atmosphere resting on an ocean so turbulent and variable; but the variety is too great and peculiar to be thus explained. The corona's spectrum of a single faint, greenish line crosses a faint continuous spectrum in which sometimes appear the absorption lines of common sunlight.

The spectrum of common sunlight is that of incandescent vapors and gases when shone through by a more heated solid or liquid, or at least by denser and hotter matter, than themselves. Just what the solar vapors and gases are is found to some extent by comparing the spectra of known substances with the solar spectrum. Not only are hydrogen and helium found in this way in the atmosphere of the Sun, but also vapors of the following metals:

Sodium,	Manganese,	Lead,
Iron,	Calcium,	Palladium,
Magnesium,	Titanium,	Strontium,
Barium,	Nickel,	Cadmium,
Copper,	Cobalt,	Aluminium,
	Uranium.	

A powerful spectroscope shows thousands of lines in the solar spectrum. Of these, less than 900 have yet been referred to known substances. Are there many elements in the earth yet undiscovered, or is the Sun largely composed of different materials from the earth? If the latter supposition is correct, the earth can hardly be a child of the Sun. Certainly some substances that enter largely into the composition of the earth (oxygen, for example, which makes up not far from half its substance) either are not found at all in the Sun or only in a slight degree.

The study of the Sun's face has brought to light some points of sympathy with the earth as well as some points of divergence. The most spots occur when the magnetic needle is most disturbed, when auroras are most striking, and when the electric currents are most powerful at the earth's surface. Between the greatest and least of all these there is a period of about eleven years.

What are the spots? After long disputes they are now generally regarded as *depressions* in the tumultuous ocean of the photosphere. At the same time it would be too much to say that no difficulties remain to this theory. Perhaps it would be mended if combined with a fuller recognition of two facts, viz., that of less bright clouds suspended over the fiery ocean and so showing darkly upon it, and that of relatively cold spots in the photosphere. Such spots must exist, must exist as depressions, must appear darker than other spots, must appear comparatively small and few at the edge of the disk and at its equator. The hotter and so the higher materials would be most drawn to the equator and so would occupy that region to the exclusion of the cooler elements.

Some scientists have undertaken to tell us *about* how old the Sun is. One says about 300,000,000 of years; another will not allow more than 18,000,000. Geologists are inclined to magnificent figures, their estimates being from 30 to 3,000 times greater than those of astronomers. On this matter we profess great ignorance. Not having the nebular hypothesis, with a lapful of sub-hypotheses, to help us out, we must submit to the mortification of saying that we do not know, even roughly, how old the Sun is. We only know that it had a beginning, that this beginning was far back beyond that of the human race, and that when it began GOD was the beginner.

Some scientists have undertaken to tell us *about* how long the fires of the Sun will last. No diminution of its light and heat has been noticed during the historic period; but it is nevertheless held by some that such a tremendous radiation as is incessantly going on must finally exhaust the supply, and the great orb hang black and frozen in the sky. That would mean awful catastrophe to us. We are concerned to know how soon we shall be frozen to death. And we are variously told that we may count on from 10,000,000 to 17,-

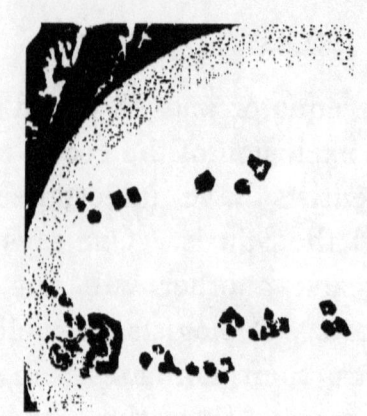

000,000 of years longer. On this matter also we profess great ignorance. We do not know how long the Sun will last. We do not even know but that it will last for ever. Have we not been hearing for years of the conservation of force? We are by no means sure that the All-wise has not hidden away amid the great compensation cycles of nature some provision for returning to the Sun all the forces it so liberally expends, as he is wont to return to the liberal man all his generosity. But one thing we are sure of, namely, that when the world comes to an end it will not be by freezing, but by conflagration. "The earth also, and the works that are therein, shall be burned up."

PLANETS. From time out of mind five of the stars have been known to be unlike the rest in that they seem to wander aimlessly about the heavens. Hence the Greeks called them planets or wanderers. And the Romans gave to each of them the proper name by which it is now known, as Mercury, Venus, Mars, Jupiter, Saturn.

I have said that astrologers have not been in the habit of viewing all the planets as friends. Jupiter and Venus were thought such; Mercury was thought friendly or otherwise according to circumstances; Mars and Saturn were dangerous. But we have recovered bravely from astrology as well as from alchemy, although in our newspapers we often see advertisements that promise great things in behalf of both these mediæval delusions, and that manage to gather a few dishonest pennies from the ignorant. But to us of riper knowledge all the planets are equally friendly, if not equally serviceable and comely. Fair Venus, morning and evening star, vision of beauty, with its gentle and caressing ray; lordly Jupiter, with its calm, majestic, and patronizing shining—we had quite as lief be born under some other planet, say thieving Mercury or bloody Mars or cannibal Saturn. It would be hard to show a single mischief any one of these has done us, while each has done something to help the heavens declare the glory of God and to illuminate the nights of the world. They are, as we shall find by-and-by, honored members of the same family, bound to us by such strong and close ties that they could not be removed without a catastrophe to us, unless a miracle should be wrought to prevent it. The fact that the old classical nations as well as others gave to them the names of their principal divinities, who were supposed to be closely related to one another, and in the main friendly to well-disposed people, shows that they were regarded as friends.

What did the ancients know about these five wandering stars? Scarcely anything, save that they wandered, some more, some less. Whether they were *ignes fatui*, bred of some celestial swamp, or sky-tramps of the better sort, or like other stars, or like the earth, their naked eyes did not inform them; and they had no other means of astronomical knowledge save that of hypothesis, on which so much stress is now being laid, and which has so often brought science into contempt. Until quite lately these planets went abroad, like Eastern dames, with veiled faces, though their veils were of silver tissue that managed to shine marvellously.

But the telescopic astronomer at length came to these shining incogs. that had for ages so jealously covered up their faces from general observation, and audaciously insisted on lifting the envious tissue. Lo, expanded orbs! Lo, earth-like bodies with atmospheres and rotations! Instead of spangles on the sky or the bright eyes of far-away spirits or miniature bonfires in the festival-keeping heavens, they appeared round worlds of earth-like matter seemingly dwarfed by distance.

MERCURY, for the most part, hides under the shining robes of the sun, never going more than 29° from it. But for a few moments before sunrise and after sunset at certain seasons it comes out of hiding and under the revealing eye of the telescope. Then we see a small disk slightly tinged with red, having a diameter nearly three times greater at some times than at others, slightly flattened at two opposite points of the disk, covered with faint spots, some of which are seen moving across the face at right angles to a line joining the flattened parts and making a complete circuit in about twenty-four hours. We also see it passing through various phases like the moon; and, as in the case of the moon, we see from the appearance of the broken edge that the surface of the planet is uneven, and, considering that it must be far from us, even mountainous. Some of these mountains are estimated to be eleven miles high. Sometimes the crescent-horns of the planet are seen extending till they meet each other and form a complete ring of light, which could not be unless the body possessed a refracting atmosphere. There seems to be evidence that this atmosphere is very dense, and that it is filled with clouds so dense that nearly nine-tenths of the light falling on it fails to reach its solid surface. The spectrum of the planet also shows that these clouds consist, in part at least, of the vapor of water, from which we infer that, like our earth, the surface in part consists of seas. The unequal reflecting powers of different substances composing the body of Mercury, the great inequalities of level, and the necessarily varying density of the cloudy envelope, sufficiently explain the spots.

It ought to be said that the nearness of Mercury to the sun so embarrasses observation that many astronomers have not been able personally to verify some of the above facts, and so hold them in doubt. But they all, after the planetary analogies and the names of Schröter, Messier, and Lemonnier, deserve some respect.

VENUS appears before the telescope with various phases and sizes similar to those of Mercury. Its apparent diameter is more than six times greater at some times than at others. Like Mercury, it is sometimes seen as a black marble, with a border, crossing the face of the sun—the famous crossing known as the Transit of Venus. Like Mercury, this planet never goes very far from the sun, though farther than Mercury. Great as are the beauty and brightness of Venus to the naked eye, they are far greater under the telescope. Hesperus and Phosphor, morning and evening star, once thought two different bodies, are now easily seen to be one, as easily as we recognize the same man in different places. The same phenomena as in the case of Mercury, if Schröter may be trusted, show that Venus has air and water and clouds and day and night about as long as our own, and great mountains, some of which bear a very considerable proportion in height to the diameter of the planet. Its atmosphere seems denser than our own. In general, however, Venus much resembles the earth.

But MARS seems to resemble the earth still more. It has within a few years been found to have moons. At a time when it was much more favorably situated for observation than it had been for a long time an American astronomer saw two points of light in the immediate neighborhood of the planet which soon showed their true character. They kept constantly moving from one side of it to the other. So we are sure they are moons. We are not quite so sure that the names given these moons, *Phobos* and *Deimos* (panic and terror), are not a little too formidable for the tiny strangers, unless, indeed, reference was had in the naming to the consternation into which one of them has thrown the nebular hypothesis by going around the planet in less than one-third of its rotation period.

For Mars rotates. By watching the stabler markings on its face we find them completing a revolution in about one of our days. And in a common telescope we see many such markings. We seem to see seas, islands, continents; and on the continental, or lighter parts, that various shading which would naturally come from variety of level and configuration. Doubtless the planet has lowlands and highlands, valleys and mountains, along which course rivulets and rivers to the seas. For the same tests that show us air, vapor of water, rapidly changing mists and clouds, and so rains and winds and storms, in Venus, show them in Mars. But what is that round white spot near the edge of the disk? As it is found matched by another on just the opposite side of the planet, and as these spots are found to occupy the poles of the planet, and also to slowly waste away as the Martial summer advances, and increase again as its winter comes on, it is certainly snow that we see.

But there are still better views of Mars. Its apparent diameter is about seven times greater at some times than at others. When it is nearest to us, and great telescopic power is brought to bear on it and it is closely watched for a considerable time, astronomers have succeeded in making quite a detailed chart of its surface. On this chart both hemispheres of the planet are shown, with water and land in their various places and proportions, but without any attempt to represent the inequalities of surface, though with a very manifest attempt to immortalize the names of certain astronomers who have figured more or less in connection with the planet. Why this ruddy hue that is given to the land? This is the tint it has even to the naked eye, and this is doubtless the reason why it received from the ancients the name of their god of war and blood. As this hue is confined to the land, it is credibly supposed to be due to the color of the soil, though thought by some to be due to the same causes as give us ruddy sunsets.

Is there no vegetation to be nourished by the soils and rains and streams of Mars; no animal to feed along its pastures, swim in its seas, or fly through its air; no superior race to enjoy its fine landscapes, its day and night, its grateful change of seasons, and its double moon?

JUPITER makes an imposing show to the naked eye. We hardly wonder as we gaze on its splendor that the Romans gave it the name of the king of their gods. But under the telescope the king is still more kingly. Is not the vertical diameter considerably shorter than the horizontal? Actual measurement shows that one is to the other as 16 is to 17. This difference leads us to suspect that Jupiter revolves at a very rapid rate on its shorter diameter. By watching certain of the more constant features of the disk, and especially a notable red spot that did not shift its position for years, it was found that the suspicion was justified and that the planet rotates in a period of about ten hours, in a plane that nearly passes through the sun, and so gives

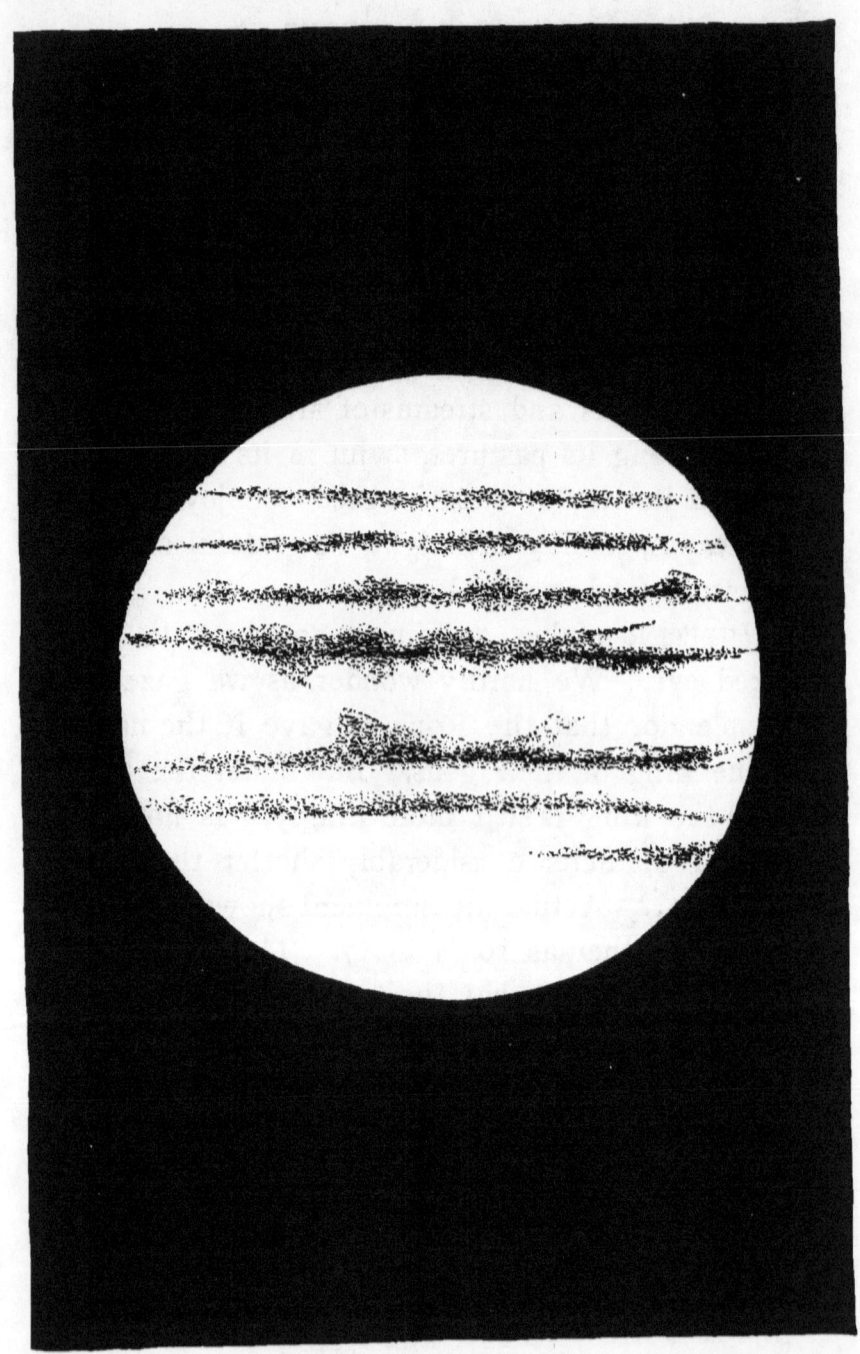

JUPITER.

nearly equal days and nights of five hours each all over its surface.

It is also found that the colored belts seen crossing the face are generally parallel to the plane of rotation. What are these belts? They are seen to undergo great and rapid changes in place, shape, size, and color. Hence it is generally supposed that they are clouds and currents drawn into parallelism with the planet's equator by its very rapid rotation. But why such immense and permanent accumulations of clouds, and why such great and rapid changes in form, place, and color? Astronomers generally suppose the cause to be an extremely heated condition of the body of the planet, raising a vast quantity of vapors and gases into the atmosphere, and variously changing them according to the various changes in the place, activity, and products of the heat-centres. This seems reasonable. Still the body of Jupiter cannot be incandescent; for its spectrum is that of reflected sunlight. It may, however, be exceptionally heated without being incandescent. It may now be in the state in which both geology and the Scriptures show that the earth once was—at once exceedingly humid and heated and so densely veiled in clouds; it may have special centres of heat and so of atmospheric disturbance; also the atmosphere itself may be very dense and peculiar in its constitution, as well as variously charged at different times and places with moisture and other outside material, and so vast masses of variously colored and changeful clouds, such as we often see at sunsets and in droughts, may easily result. If this is the true explanation of the belts of Jupiter, the nebular hypothesis in its earlier form has another difficulty to explain, viz., how one of the first formed planets has not cooled down as much as vastly later ones.

This difficulty has seemed insuperable to many evolutionists. Accordingly Spencer and others, giving up the original form of the hypothesis, suggest another which supposes that a comparatively cool mass of extremely diffused gases and vapors in rotating broke up into several thin concentric rings at about the same time, and that the interior rings graduated into worlds sooner than the exterior. But this view is weighted with special difficulties of its own—as may be noticed elsewhere. It is not the easiest thing in the world to conceive how a rotating body can throw off several rings at about the same time, or how the hottest of these rings could cool off into a habitable world some millions of years in advance of the coldest.

But the most interesting fact connected with

Jupiter, and the very first revealed by the telescope, is the fact that the planet has a family of four bright stars revolving about it. They approach it, cross its face, pass beyond a little way, then return, disappear behind it, reappear, and go on to the first position. They are evidently satellites, moons—very small in comparison with their primary. The nearest completes a circuit in forty-two hours; the most remote in about two weeks; the others in times between these. They resemble our moon also in that each rotates and completes a rotation in the same time in which it circles about the planet. An opera-glass will show them. By means of these satellites the velocity of light was first discovered; and this discovery was so brilliant and useful that we shall always be thankful to the little ones whose "hide and seek" about their illustrious father gave it to us, though we now have more accurate sources of information.

Though not very brilliant to the naked eye, SATURN was known from the earliest times, not only as a wanderer, but as one that, like Jupiter and Mars, wandered away from the sun by the whole breadth of the sky. But as to the features of old *Chronos*—none knew anything of them till the telescope with its great, calm eye shot searching and persistent gaze upon it. That gaze revealed a mottled orb revolving on itself in about twelve hours, crossed by permanent yet changeable belts parallel to its plane of rotation, after the manner of Jupiter, and arguing, as is supposed, the same physical condition with that planet as to exceeding heat and moisture; revealed also that the axis of rotation is considerably inclined to a line joining Saturn with the sun, and consequently causes at any given point on its surface unequal days and nights.

But the chief interest of Saturn lies in its ring and great family of eight moons. The discovery of the ring made a great stir among astronomers, and much speculation, which has hardly yet settled into science. When first seen by Galileo the ring was in such a position that it seemed two handles, as it were, to the planet; but, in course of time, it came to be seen as shown elsewhere. We see that the ring appears multiple, is parallel with the belts, which are themselves found parallel with the plane of rotation. It is sometimes edgewise to us and then is not seen at all; so that its thickness must be very small compared with its width—not more than 50 or 100 miles. Indeed, the innermost ring of all is so thin as to be transparent. What is this strange appendage? It is thought that the observations are best satisfied by supposing that it consists of

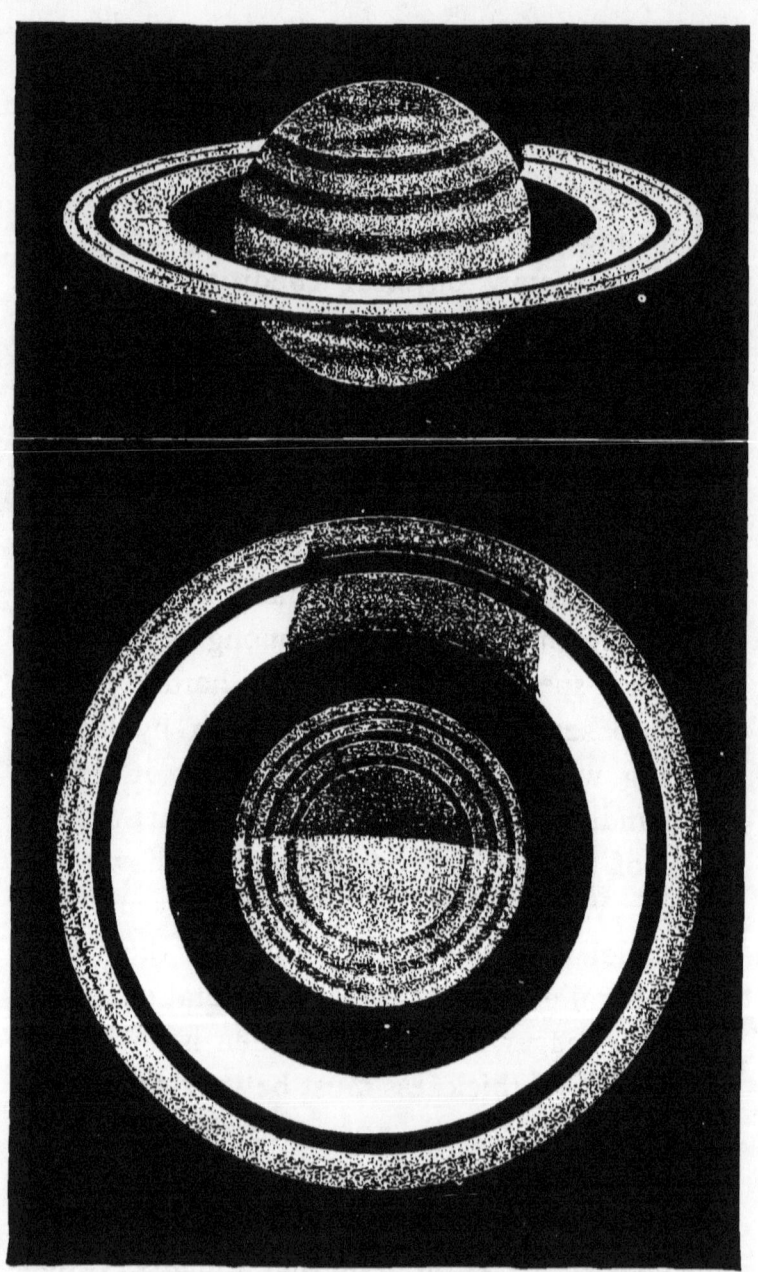

SATURN AND ITS RINGS.

many thin concentric zones of minute, discrete, aëriform bodies, almost like flakes of snow, circulating about the planet—crowded in some parts and comparatively diffuse in others, and at any given point varying much in aspect from changes in the density of the zone at that point. If this hypothesis is correct—if the ring is really a series of concentric disks whose thickness in comparison with their breadth is nearly inappreciable, and the innermost ring the least dense of all, we have other embarrassments to the nebular hypothesis in whatever form—in addition to that which the original form has—in that the aspects of Saturn, like those of Jupiter, seem to show that it is vastly less advanced than the earth was millions of years ago. It is hard to see how disks of such thinness could be thrown off by a rotating planet under any circumstances, especially by a planet whose rotation-period even now is about ten hours; or how, when once thrown off, it could divide up its continuous cloudy material into myriads of separate flakes, and gradually thin out, from such a figure as one would get by cutting off from the equatorial regions of the planet enough to leave it a perfect globe, to such extreme and filmy thinness and even transparency as we observe.

Time out of mind have appeared in the sky

certain objects which from their hairy aspect have been called COMETS. These bodies, so far from being viewed as friends, have generally been regarded with alarm, and often with terror. They meant public disaster. Famine, pestilence, war, all sorts of wide-spread ruin, were supposed to be presaged by them. It was not known what their constitution was or what laws governed them.

An object very unlike any other in the whole sky was suddenly noticed. It had a roundish head in which sometimes appeared a nucleus; and generally, streaming away from this in a direction opposite the sun, a tail or tails of extremely varying form and size, sometimes mere zero, and sometimes stretching over a third of the heavens. After waxing for a time in size and brightness it gradually waned, and in a short time had disappeared altogether. Where has it gone? Will it ever reappear? "Let us hope not," said the ancient public; "let us hope not, thou prophet of evil, thou bird of ill-omen, thou terror of the nations, thou enemy of mankind."

But we have gradually come to pleasanter views of things. Comets were found quite as apt to forerun prosperities as adversities. The public now gazes on one with great self-possession. Even little children never turn pale as they look up at the spectral visitor. And astronomers joyfully

1 AND 5 HALLEY'S COMET AT DIFFERENT TIMES.
2 AND 3 DONATI'S COMET AT DIFFERENT TIMES.
4 COMET OF 1843.

welcome him—the bigger and fiercer-looking the better. They push out their telescopes from a hundred watch-towers, study every feature with great interest, tell how long it has been since his last visit, ask when he will come again. They are not afraid of him, know of no harm that he or his comrades have done, think him a pleasant variety in the celestial scenery, know that he has already brought us valuable news from far-distant regions, and hope that some day, mighty traveller as he is, he will bring us still more. From behind no one of the thousand telescopes levelled at him beams an unwelcoming eye.

And the following facts have been learned. Comets consist of gaseous matter, sometimes so extremely diffused that faint stars can be seen through their densest parts. As they approach the sun they naturally brighten and expand with the increasing heat; then they recede in these respects as they recede from the sun. As to the elements composing them, the spectroscope has examined several and found that they consist each of a single element; that in the case of at least two the elements are such as have not yet been recognized as terrestrial, and that of two others, one consists of nitrogen and the other of carbon. It is also generally conceded by evolutionists that the comets cannot be regarded as children of the sun by natural genesis, as their more solid fellow-wanderers have been credited with being.

That these occasional ghostly visitors serve some valuable purpose in the economy of the heavens we are bound to believe. But what that is as yet baffles our science. If "all things come to him who waits," this will come among them.

OTHER BODIES. The ancients noticed occasional meteorites and meteors—the first being fireballs moving near the earth, and sooner or later reaching it, commonly after the explosion; the second being what are familiarly known as shooting stars.

Notwithstanding the alarm sometimes excited by the sudden appearance and detonations of meteorites, intelligent men are always glad to know of them and to get specimens for their museums. When examined microscopically and chemically these specimens are all found to consist of like materials, though differently combined, viz., iron and some compounds of silica with various metals and other substances. The structure seems to indicate an original state of fusion, and as some think even of gas. Did they come from the glowing furnaces which we know to exist in the bowels of the earth, and which sometimes take voice in earthquakes and volcanoes? The elements are all such as belong to the earth;

and though they are not found at the surface in the same combinations, in the great crucibles and under the immense pressures of the interior there is abundant explanation of all things possible to heat and condensation. This explanation may sufsuffice for some fire-balls that have been noticed. But there are others for which it will not suffice. Often when first observed they are some 80 or 90 miles above the earth and moving obliquely towards it, which is inconsistent with the idea that they do not come from without our atmosphere. At present astronomers are agreed that in general both meteorites and meteors are extra-terrene bodies; that they are of substantially the same material, as shown by their spectra; and that meteors, especially the meteoric showers in April, August, and November, are nearly related to comets, and move in clouds about the sun.

Each of the familiar celestial objects just described (earth, moon, sun, five planets, comets, etc.) appears so different to us from what it did to the ancients that it may be said to have been *transformed* by modern research. And they have also been transformed collectively as well as individually. What were once supposed to have no closer relation to us and to one another than have the other heavenly bodies, are now known to be relatively our neighbors. This is inferable from the fact that their apparent motions greatly exceed all others in the sky. They must be comparatively near us. A far greater space must part them from the other stars than parts them from us and from one another. We are a family wholly by ourselves.

And this celestial family has been gradually transformed in another respect—in respect to apparent size. The few ancient "wanderers" have become many modern ones. During the last century hundreds have been added to our list, notably Uranus and Neptune, the former with four moons, and the latter with one; the former visible to the naked eye as a faint star, and the latter visible only to the telescope. The discovery of these new planets created great surprise. All the others just mentioned had been known for thousands of years. It was even maintained by the astronomical fathers that there *could* be no more. Did not the sun, moon, and five planets complete the sacred number seven? That was conclusive. So when Herschel, in 1781, detected a small greenish disk lurking among stars of the sixth magnitude, and moving about in a small way, a thrill of astonishment and enthusiasm ran through the whole scientific world. But still greater and wider enthusiasm was felt when, in 1846, Neptune was discovered. This because of the manner of its discovery. The motions of Uranus were found disturbed. Where must a new planet have been and now be to produce this disturbance? Two astronomers suggested a place in the sky. The telescope was pointed to it, and lo, *Neptune!*

In addition to these, considerably more than two hundred faint planets have been found nestling in our group. Though plainly neighbors, and much nearer than some of the other planets—as is shown by their much greater apparent motion—none of them show sensible disks under the largest telescopes. It follows that they are comparatively small objects. Accordingly they have been called planetoids or asteroids. Proper names, however, have been given to all of them.

Thus certain of the most familiar objects in the old-time heavens have in the course of modern research been transformed both individually and collectively. The features of each have been read after a manner that would have astonished the ancients; they have all been found neighbors to one another as compared with the fixed stars; and this neighborhood has been found shared by many associates whose very existence until lately was quite unsuspected. So we have what is known as THE SOLAR SYSTEM.

V. NUMBERS.

1. NEW NEIGHBORS.
2. DOUBLE AND MULTIPLE STARS.
3. MILKY WAY.
4. OTHER GALAXIES.

V. NUMBERS.

ASTRONOMICAL instruments have done much more than enlarge our acquaintance with certain celestial objects already familiar. They have drawn aside a veil and revealed to us a host of objects in the sky which until lately never met the gaze of the sharpest eyes.

A vague look at the heavens has always given the impression of almost innumerable stars. But actual count with the naked eye individualizes only about 5,000 in both hemispheres. When, however, we bring a telescope of even a low power to bear heavenward we discover objects that during all the past have been total strangers to men; and, as we increase our optical powers, the few golden seeds scattered over the sky-fields gradually ripen into a harvest that is absolutely amazing.

First, as we have seen, we discover an addition of some hundreds to that family of neighbor orbs to which we belong, and which, out of deference to the brightest object among them, we have called the solar system. As about half a score of new asteroids have been found annually for now many years, we are entitled to expect that more will be found.

Turning now a telescope on the fixed stars, we find some that appear single to the naked eye becoming double, triple, quadruple, sextuple. One, *Theta Orionis*, is found to consist of seven stars. About 6,000 of these multiple objects have been noticed. What seemed a small group turns out to be a cluster of scores or hundreds or thousands. Thus the six or seven stars commonly noticed in the Pleiades become sixty or more, and yonder white spot, about one-tenth the apparent size of the moon, becomes the famous cluster in Hercules, with, perhaps, 30,000 stars. Vacant spaces become populous, one star becomes many, groups become clusters, small clusters become shining armies, the Milky Way—and what of the Milky Way? What is that luminous or sub-luminous cloud that belts our heavens? The unaided eye has no answer ready, whatever the imagination may suspect. But look into a certain mammoth reflector and you will find the riddle of the ages read out loudly into your vernacular, as you see some 18,000,000 of distinct stars, instead of the milk which baby Hercules spilled of old or the celestial snow-banks of a moment ago.

The telescope notices, mostly in a zone at right angles to the Milky Way and about its

THE MILKY WAY.

poles, not far from 6,000 cloud-like objects, hence called *nebulæ*. They are of all apparent sizes, from a diameter of twenty degrees downwards. Sometimes they are far apart—lone islands in great oceans of space, and sometimes, like the stars, they are gathered into neighborhoods of two, three, or more. Huge archipelagos of them are found in the constellation Virgo. As to shape there is very great variety. Some are circular, some oval, some annular, and some consist of concentric rings. One resembles a crab, another a dumb-bell, still another an hour-glass. There are fans and spirals and whirlpools, plumes, banners, and swords. Some have a uniform brightness throughout, others are spotted with nuclei, others fade away gradually from centre to outskirts, while still others have ragged, vacant patches within; in short, they differ among themselves in form and aspect almost as do the clouds of our atmosphere. What are they?

By far the greater part of these faint celestial mists and snows have been resolved into stars. If these resolved nebulæ are other Milky Ways, as astronomers commonly suppose, and if each of them has on the average as large a stellar census as the Milky Way, we have within reach of our telescopes not far from 100,000 millions of stars. And each of these stars, as we shall see further on, implies many invisible bodies in its neighborhood, such as we know under the name of planets. What a sum total!

But is this all? Have the heavens given any sign of coming exhaustion as we have swept into them deeper and deeper with our expanding refractors and reflectors? We have now passed from an eye of one-quarter-inch diameter to one of 72 inches by, say a hundred, successive enlargements, and each enlargement up to the present has not only brought into view new stars, but has proved as rich a discoverer as its immediate predecessor. Of course we are courageous as to the future. We confidently expect that the past will repeat itself. Does the universe come to an end just at the point where our present glasses happen to fail us? We will not be so unphilosophic as to say, Yes. It is vastly probable that we need to make a vast addition to the magnificent total of stars actually seen by our telescopes, giving a whole that is wonderful, confounding, and practically infinite to us. Never hunting-grounds so rich in game as those vast preserves on high where the telescope is the mighty Nimrod. Never deeps turning out such net-breaking multitudes as those deeps and heights over our heads into which our telescopic net has swept a little here and there and come out almost broken with its shining freight. Never in all our populous Indias and Chinas such a census as the astronomer can safely forecast after having looked over only a small part of that grand cerulean empire whose frontiers are far beyond the eye of the largest telescope. Yes, practically infinite is the number of the stars. What our glasses have yet discovered are merely the outposts of unseen armies that defy computation.

But we are not allowed to stop even here. What if the practical infinity is *absolute* infinity? We are bound to take into account the *possibility* that infinite space contains an absolutely infinite population of stars. Who is in a condition to deny this? It is demonstrable, as Sir John Herschel has shown, that while an infinite number of stars sown at hap-hazard through space would give a milky aspect to the whole heavens, such would not be the effect if they are arranged in certain conceivable systems—in fact, in such systems as actually exist. The general sky would appear as it does now, though the endless room has endless occupancy. But what does an absolute infinity of stars mean? Set down a figure—say 9. Now annex to this another like figure, and to this another still, and so on, figure after figure, till you have hundreds, thousands, millions, billions, trillions of them; keep on doing this till you have worn away years, lifetimes, the lives of nations and dispensations and worlds, in industrious and unintermitted figure-making.; keep on doing it till you have a line of figures so long that the fleetest angel that ever shook tempestuous wing across the spaces could not fly over its whole length in all his immortal years, and let such a line stand for a mere suggestion of the infinite stars.

"So many as the stars of the sky in multitude and as the sands on the seashore innumerable." The sands on all shores would be a terrible task to an accountant. Whoever should set himself to count the leaves of all lands "when summer is green or when autumn has blown" would be as much of a madman or a fool as one would care to see. Even the animals of the world, great and small, so crowd in their millions on air and water and land, and even into the deep foundations of the earth (does not a cubic inch of Bilin polishing-slate contain the silicious shells of 40,000,000 of Galeonellæ?), that an invitation to name or even to count all their individuals would almost seem an invitation to become God. Such quite would be an invitation to count the number of the stars—certain, probable, and possible. Omniscience alone suffices for such a task. "He telleth the number of the stars; he calleth them all by their names." Cyrus the elder is said to have known each soldier in his army by name. We are not told how large his army was; but this we know, that if it numbered a few hundred thousands the story is absurdly incredible. But it is not incredible that the Infinite should comprehend the infinite, that the Great King who made and owns and marshals all the starry armies should have a minute acquaintance with every single individual among them, though sown as thickly through all the immensities as are fireflies through a summer's eve or as wheat-seeds on the banks of the Euxine.

So the telescope deserves to be called the Columbus of the heavens, for, like the other Tuscan, it is a very great discoverer.

So the telescope is like the "Great Eastern," for it carries cables of communication across oceans, joins us in knowledge and sympathy with countless regions beyond, and gives us nightly the privilege of communing with them, though at something less than a dollar a word.

So the telescope is *not* wholly like the famous "Challengers" which of late years have gone dredging through our watery deeps with such success that we are not without hope that the time is not far distant when our whole sea-bottom will have reasonably well given up its secrets. The sky is a deeper deep and a wider, so deep and wide that we are quite hopeless that we will ever touch bottom as our telescopes go sounding along the celestial abysses. But they have brought up from the shallower depths of that great azure ocean so many shining things as tax beyond measure our powers of numeration, and tell of inexhaustible riches awaiting longer lines and heavier plummets and a grander courage.

VI. DISTANCES.

1. APPARENT.
2. LUNAR AND SOLAR.
3. PLANETARY.
4. STELLAR.
5. ULTIMATE TELESCOPIC.
6. ULTIMATE.

VI. DISTANCES.

If a child is taken out under the evening sky and asked how far away he thinks the heavenly bodies to be, he is not unlikely to say that they are all at about the same distance from him, and that not a very great one—say the distance of yonder house or hill. Those astronomical children whom we call the ancients generally took the same view. The Latin and Greek poets conceived of the summit of Olympus in Thessaly as being above the stars, and that, consequently, the gods in descending to the earth had to pass by the stars. And, till within a few hundred years, even the scholars of the world have held that the astronomical distances, though differing somewhat, are all of them quite inconsiderable. And by far the larger part of mankind still take the same view.

The friends of Job were not remarkable for just views of things. But one of them was very correct when he exclaimed, *Behold the stars, how high they are!* We can tell the real heights, that is, the real distances, of the moon and sun from us by noticing how much they are displaced on the sky by a given change of place on our part. In this way we find that the moon is a matter of 240,000 miles away. To a man accustomed to measure his work by a two-foot rule, and who steps at the rate of three miles an hour, this distance is something embarrassing even to the conception. But when a like process gives us about 91,000,000 of miles as the distance of the sun from us, we begin to think lightly of lunar distances, and to feel the necessity for larger units of measure than miles to help our thought to travel intelligently across such immense spaces. Think of the lifetimes that would have to be consumed in travelling to the sun by any vehicles known to us!

Knowing the distance of the sun from the earth, we can find the distances of two other planets, Mercury and Venus, from the sun, as well as from ourselves, by simply noticing their greatest angular distances from that body. These distances, as well as those of all the other planets, may also be found by the method of parallax that is used for the sun and moon, also by observing the daily apparent motions of the planets and reducing them to what they would be as viewed from the sun. The simplest trigonometry suffices for an approximation, though the most difficult mathematics are needed for great accuracy. No-

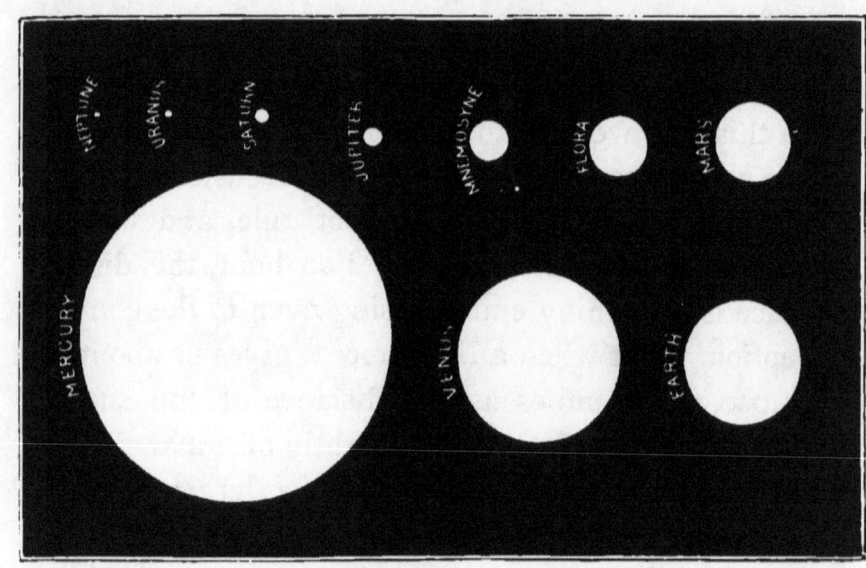

COMPARATIVE SIZE OF THE SUN AS SEEN FROM DIFFERENT PLANETS.

PHASES OF VENUS FOR ONE YEAR.

tice the distances of the chief planets from the sun—roughly approximate:

	Miles.		Miles.
Mercury,	35,000,000	Jupiter,	476,000,000
Venus,	66,000,000	Saturn,	872,000,000
Earth,	91,000,000	Uranus,	1,752,000,000
Mars,	139,000,000	Neptune,	2,746,000,000

All the asteroids are situated between Mars and Jupiter at an average distance from the sun of 260,000,000 of miles. How happened it that every nebulous zone cast off from the sun, with a single exception, settled into one orb, while that between Mars and Jupiter settled into several hundreds?

Of course the distances of the other planets from the earth, though numerically different from those just given, are of the same general order of magnitude.

Thus far we have been ascending a ladder, and at each step have come to a wider outlook on the great spaces of the creation. Can we mount still higher and see still farther? What of the fixed stars, so called? How far from us are they?

It was not till quite lately that the beginning of an answer could be given to this question. But by noting with extreme care the places of certain stars at an interval of six months (that is at points 180 millions of miles apart) we have found minute changes of position which, when combined with our distance from the sun, give approximately their distances from it and us. More than twenty stars have thus been made to report themselves. See some of the astonishing figures:

Alpha Centauri,	224,000	sun distances.
61 Cygni,	366,000	"
1830 Groombridge,	912,000	"
70 Ophiuchi,	1,286,000	"
Vega,	1,337,000	"
Sirius,	1,375,000	"
Arcturus,	1,624,000	"
Polaris,	3,078,000	"
Capella,	4,484,000	"

Not one of the fixed stars thus far heard from is away from us less then 200,000 times 91 millions of miles.

In the foregoing list Polaris is the most interesting object, though neither the brightest nor the most remote. Ever since men began they have been guiding their wanderings on sea and land by the North Star. And little aware have the travellers been that they were being guided by light which had come for that purpose across so vast an interval. Most of them would have been sure that an average steam-car rate of motion would bring them to the star in a short time. Suppose one to set out. He goes on a straight line, goes night and day without stopping, goes at the rate of 20 miles an hour for 500 years. At the end of this time he has accomplished one sun-distance, one stage in his journey, and yet as he looks there is no perceptible increase of light in the star. This is discouraging. But, after all, what are 500 years to an immortal? So he plucks up heart and starts again. This time he goes steadily on for a period equal to the whole past of our race on the earth. Six thousand years of incessant rush are at last behind him, and he stops again to take account of progress. He looks at the star. It has still no sensible diameter, and it would be hard to say that it is even a thought brighter than it was of old. It is still a star of the third magnitude. Shall he go on? He hesitates. He thinks he does well to hesitate. Thirteen milestones have been passed; but then more than three million others remain. Evidently, he has hardly made a beginning. Evidently, no impression worth mentioning is yet made on the mighty interval he has undertaken to wear away. Why, at such a rate of progress it will take more than 1,500 millions of years still to reach the goal. Can even an immortal afford such an outlay? Fifteen hundred millions of years! Fancy tires at the very idea. "No, it cannot be afforded. Unless he can have a far swifter vehicle than he has been using, unless the light itself can be persuaded to be his steed, or some angel, such as ever and anon shoots by him, will be kind enough to take him on his wings, he must give up the undertaking." We applaud his decision. But there is yet another round to our upward-going ladder. Unless we suppose that all the larger stars lie nearest to us (which is not to be supposed), we must admit that the average size of the 5,000 stars visible to the naked eye is probably not much different from that of the next 5,000 brought into view by some telescope, or any other 5,000 brought into view by successive enlargements of the telescopic power until we have an instrument commanding a stellar population of some 18,000,000. It follows that the average brightness to us of these successive strata of stars depends solely on their distance from us, according to the well-known law that the brightness of an object diminishes as the square of its distance from the observer increases. But the nearest star, Alpha Centauri, if carried away from us so far as to be only equally bright in our largest telescope, would be about 25,000,000 times farther from us than it now is, and in order to be just visible in that telescope would have to be much farther away.

But there are thousands of stars just brought into view by the great Rossian reflector. Now Alpha Centauri, as we have seen, is nearly four years from us as flies the light. Think of stars so distant that their light has been more than 75,000,000 of years in coming to us, though travelling without intermission at the rate of 186,000 miles a second!

But there must be stars still more distant; for as, up to the present, each successive enlargement of the telescope has brought new stars into view without any sign of their number being exhausted or abated, we are authorized to expect that further enlargement will give further discoveries. And where is the final frontier and last picket of the heavenly host? It is plain to every astronomer that his thought is summoned away to stars posted amazing stretches beyond the present boundaries of vision, however grandly helped that vision is by optical art. Indeed, as space is absolutely infinite, who can say that there *is* any last star, any bright point where our jaded thought can fold its wing and say, "Ah, what a mighty travel it has been! but it is finished at last. All nature is now behind me—nothing but stark nothingness before me. I look off into the awful blackness of utter vacancy. Could I set up the Rossian tube on this outward-looking rampart, not a single ray could it gather from the whole mighty night towards which it gazes."

Such are the distances of the fixed stars from us. How far are they from one another? By means of the actual distances of any two stars from us, and the apparent interval between them, we can easily compute the real interval. This has never been found less than 1,000 millions of miles, about ten times our distance from the sun, which is the distance between the two stars of Zeta Herculis. And there is many another star whose nearest star-neighbor is almost infinitely farther away.

Robin of the Longbow could send an arrow wonderfully far. Far-shooting Apollo, Homer being witness, could send one much farther. But even Apollo was under the necessity of taking a position within moderate distance of his target. But yonder celestial archers defy distance. It counts for just nothing to such long bows and strong bows as theirs. They shoot light at us and at one another across unimaginable universes. The silver shafts come flying to us from the other side of the creation (is there the other side?) without the least loss of speed, and hit their mark every time. This, however, we must confess they would not do if they did not shoot arrows by millions instead of by units.

Preposterous neighbors! Individuals and nations are often cramped by their narrow quarters, and break away in impetuous rivers of emigration into roomy Americas and Australias, where they can get breath and elbow-room and have full scope for their faculties and industries and enterprises. Surely the stars have no need to emigrate. However crowded together they may seem by distance and by visual superposition, they have no occasion to say, "The place is too strait for me; give place to me that I may dwell." Who was it that said, "An ocean between peoples is a great peacemaker"? If this is so, the stars are under heavy bonds to keep the peace. What stupendous Atlantics and Pacifics part them! Space is awfully plentiful. Enough of it has been given to each star to satisfy the largest appetite for loneliness and liberty. Do they need it that their vagaries and eccentricities may not disturb one another? How quiet and orderly they seem. One could think them hermit-saints, who have retired, each into his own nook of the vast azure wilderness, to escape temptation, to pray and fast and be alone with God. But perhaps they are not the stark hermits, and unsocial though bright-faced anchorites, that they seem. Is it not just possible that they have about them clans of retainers, families of children, which on account of their smallness or dimness cannot be seen by us? Oases in the widest desert we know of—bright islets frugally sown in a boundless sea! let us hope that you do not want for that most necessary thing, congenial companionship of your own species!

The questions are sometimes asked, How old is the earth? How long since the solar system was started? How far back that "beginning" of which our Scriptures speak in their opening sentence, "In the beginning God created the heavens and the earth"? Men of science have tried to answer the first two questions in a rough, *very* rough way, with vast differences between themselves, and especially between geologists and astronomers; but the last question has seemed almost too formidable to be grappled with, audacious as is modern speculation. Yet in view of what has been said of the exceeding distances of some of the stars, we can make a small contribution towards an answer. Inasmuch as there are some stars so far away that their light has been hundreds of millions of years in coming to us, the first creation of vast masses of matter must have been at least hundreds of millions of years back. How much farther who can say?

VII. SIZES.

1. APPARENT.
2. AMONG THE NEAR.
3. AMONG THE FAR.
4. THE GIANT.

VII. SIZES.

THE ancients generally thought the apparent size of the moon, sun, planets, and stars fairly represented their real size. So children and uncivilized men think now. To them the stars pass for luminous points, bright grains of sand; and as for the sun and moon, they set them down at a venture as equal to an average human head. Occasionally an ancient scientist, like Anaxagoras, thought that the sun and moon might be each as large as the Peloponnesus. Somewhat larger ideas were sometimes ventured upon, and we are told that Anaximander, who lived some 600 years before Christ, thought that the moon was about nineteen times and the sun about twenty-seven times larger than the earth. But all such ideas were mere guesses and far astray from the current opinion even among the cultured.

But just as soon as accurate instruments had made it possible to find accurately the places of the heavenly bodies, and it had been found that their displacement on the sky was very trifling for great changes in the position of the observer—that is to say, when it was found that their distance from us was immense—then it began to be felt that their size must be immense also. Thus, as soon as it was known that the displacement of the moon from going a whole half-diameter of the earth at right angles to the moon's direction was about 57', and so it became known that its distance from us must be about 237,000 miles, it was known that its real diameter must be about 2,100 miles. In the same way we may find the diameters of all the other heavenly bodies which have apparent diameters in the telescope. They are as follows:

	Miles.		Miles.
Mercury .	2,900.	Jupiter . .	85,000.
Venus . .	7,500.	Saturn . .	72,000.
Earth . .	7,900.	Uranus . .	33,000.
Mars . . .	4,900.	Neptune .	37,000.

The asteroids and some of the planetary moons show no sensible disks in even the largest telescopes, so that we have to judge of their size from their relative brightness. According to this the diameters of the asteroids vary from 128 miles to less than 50, those of the satellites from 3,300 miles in the case of one of the satellites of Jupiter, to less than 10 miles in the case of the two moons belonging to Mars. But the Sun is the wonder for size, for at the distance of 91,000,000 of miles from us its apparent diameter means a real one of 852,000 miles.

But what are the sizes of the fixed stars? Here a difficulty arises. These objects have no measurable diameters in our telescopes, however powerful; and so, even when their distances are known, their real diameters cannot be found in the way just mentioned. Here the instrument called the photometer comes into play. What would be the brightness of the sun at the distance of Alpha Centauri? This question is easily answered by means of the law that the light of a given object diminishes as the square of its distance from the observer increases. And we find that the brightness of this star is twice what our sun would have at the same distance. In the same way we find that Sirius is equal to 63 suns, Polaris to 86, Capella to 430, Arcturus to 516, Alcyone to 12,000. But we remember that our sun is 852,000 miles in diameter. The unit with which we have compared the above stars is itself a gigantic thing. Think of a disk like Alcyone's that gives the light of 12,000 suns, and whose diameter, therefore, must be more than one hundred times that of our sun! What a day that star would make for us if substituted for our sun! We should need different eyes from our present ones, it is plain; and, if the heat is proportioned to the light, we should need different bodies throughout, also a different world, for 12,000 times our greatest summer heat would melt down everything and convert it into gas. Twelve thousand equatorial days condensed into one would have a terrible significance to the most salamandrine nature known on this world of ours.

So we see that the huge distances of the sky are marked by huge milestones. The great country above is occupied by giant inhabitants, Anakim whose stature is so great that their shining shields can be seen across an almost limitless ocean. Ye who admire great stature, and would go, it may be, hundreds of miles to see a man twelve feet high, look up where you are and wonder at the mighty forms that nightly look down on us from the populous heavens. Certainly our little world makes a very humble appearance in the presence of such stupendous colossi—much more do our petty kingdoms, principalities, and estates. How Russia and Great Britain and the United States, on occasion, can boast of their far-stretching parallels and meridians! How even individual proprietors in these lands will flush themselves on the idea of possessing a few thousand acres of land, together with a few castles and manor houses and city blocks! Behold the vast estates and palaces and cities and kingdoms of the Proprietor of proprietors!

VIII. NATURES.

1. ANCIENT GUESSES.
2. MODERN CERTAINTIES.
3. EARTHS AND SUNS.
4. PLANETARY CENTRES.
5. NEBULÆ AS SUNS.

VIII. NATURES

WE have seen what the ancients largely thought about the nature of the sun, moon, and planets, and how widely their views differed from the true. A like difference is found in regard to the fixed stars. "They are luminous exhalations from the earth, like the *ignes fatui* over marshes," said some. "They are spangles of various sizes fastened to the inside of a hollow azure sphere," thought others. Others still, perhaps, were disposed to think that they were golden grains, heavenly eyes, the camp-fires of celestial hosts, or openings through the sphere into a glory beyond. The majority in rude ages and countries, familiar with the heavens from infancy and pressed by their daily toils and needs, probably never fairly thought about the matter at all— never troubled themselves to form a theory of the nature of objects so aloof from their current lives, or imagined them to be the lesser among their innumerable divinities. Similar ideas and ignorances are found to-day in some countries.

And yet, all through the ages, wiser opinions have now and then found expression. Thales, who lived more than six centuries before Christ, held that the stars were of the same substance as the earth, but in a state of ignition. And this view was continued for some time in the Ionian School which Thales founded.

But what has the latest science to say as to the nature of the fixed stars? We have already seen that they are all objects at a vast remove from us, and consequently must be of vast size; and we have even made such precise determinations of some of these vast distances and sizes as strain our powers of expression and conception. As the spherical form is that to which all bodies are observed to tend under the influence of gravitation, and as the sun and moon and planets are substantially spheres, we conclude that the fixed stars are spheres also. But what makes them shine? Are they not, like our sun, vast worlds on fire? As much is hinted to us by the *thermo-multiplier*, which reports heat in all the brighter stars. But the spectroscope answers more largely.

It tells us that Virgil built better than he knew when he built the stately verse:

> "Vos, æterni ignes, et non violabile vestrum
> Testor numen."

It tells us that the stars are self-luminous; that their light is of an incandescent body; that it is in general the light of a comparatively solid and bright interior shining through an atmosphere of glowing gas or vapor; also, that these gases or vapors are, some of them, like those found on the earth, while others are unknown; that each orb has its peculiarity of constitution both as to the nature and proportion of its chemical elements. This difference of constitution, as well of stage of ignition, is suggested by a difference in general color. Some stars are white, some red, some blue, some green—in short, all the colors are represented. But even those of the same general color to the eye give different spectra, and the same star sometimes gradually changes its color in the course of long periods. Thus Sirius has changed from red to green.

So it is now found, what Kepler suspected and ventured to guess in writing, viz., that the stars are suns. If so, has not each one, like our sun, a system of planets revolving about it?

The time may come when direct observation can answer this question affirmatively. Already the minute companions of several double stars have come under suspicion as shining by reflected light. But we want something more than suspicion; and, somehow, more has been obtained. Astronomers are a unit in the belief that each fixed star is the centre of a planetary group. And they are not troubled in this belief by the fact that it is not as yet decisively confirmed by direct observation. They say to themselves, "It is not strange that bodies relatively so small as all observed planets are, and shining by comparatively feeble reflected light, should as yet fail to report themselves clearly in our instruments across such immense spaces as separate us from the region of the fixed stars."

But whence this universal positive belief among astronomers? There is absolutely nothing against it. All analogy is for it. As point after point of likeness to our sun (as to size, ignition, material, gravity, motion) has gradually come to our knowledge, we have of course been logically drawn to look with more and more favor on the idea that the likeness extends still farther and that the stars resemble the sun in the office it fulfils as the centre of light and heat and revolution to neighboring planets. We find 61 Cygni trembling in its orbit as if disturbed by unseen neighbors. The readiest explanation of the variable stars is that, like our sun, they have spots which sympathize in some blind way with the movements of bodies in their vicinity. But perhaps the most fruitful source of the current belief is in that general course of astronomical experience and observation the particulars of which are too minute and shadowy for individual presentation, or even distinct conception, but which at last sum up so heavily as to argue like a king. As we cannot individualize the particles of dew, though at last the fleece becomes wringing wet; as we cannot separate the stars in certain nebulæ, though the accumulation of them brightly whitens the field of the telescope; so to one largely conversant with the heavens have come gradually countless subtle suggestions which singly are hardly distinguishable, much less presentable in words, but which at last come to be enough to saturate the thought with the conviction that every star has its cortége of dependent orbs. In this way astronomers have come to be practically unanimous in allowing that the fixed stars represent as many groups of worlds like that belonging to our sun. The friends of the nebular hypothesis are also forced to this by their view of the manner in which the stars were formed; while astronomers who believe in final causes and ascribe the stars directly to the Supernatural are also forced to it by their view of what might be expected from the Supreme Being. What considerable use can the stars subserve save as suns to other worlds? for surely they were not made in vain, or merely to make our nights somewhat more picturesque. Is it not justly inferable from the divine wisdom and goodness that yonder vast centres of light and heat and force have about them worlds to utilize their vast resources? To suppose the contrary is to suppose that nature is comparatively a waste, and to subtract greatly from our conception of the empire of God — which is contrary to the whole drift of modern discovery. And so, what with this reason or with that, astronomers hold that the solar system is but a single example of arrangements that exist through the whole realm of astronomy.

This then is the nature of the fixed stars. They are vast worlds; they are vast worlds on fire, i. e., suns; they are vast suns composed of various elements, some of which belong to the earth; they are vast suns, each of which is the centre of a planetary system.

But what of those nebulæ which have not yet been resolved into stars? These are variously estimated at from one-third to one-tenth of the whole number. While some astronomers suppose that these, like their fellows, are made up of discrete stars which would appear as such in more powerful instruments than we have at present, others suppose that they are vast, continuous masses of incandescent gas destined to finally ripen into planets and suns. The reasons assigned for this latter view are principally three: first, the known existence in space of extremely tenuous and diffused material in the form of comets and meteoric systems; second, the forms which some nebulæ have and which are such as fire-mists would naturally take on their way to planets and satellites and suns—e. g., a spherical cloud with a central nucleus, a nucleus surrounded by a ring or rings, rings with nuclei of special brightness in them, a nebulous star; third, the gaseous spectra given by some of the nebulæ. To this it is answered that comets are never incandescent save when near the sun; that some of the nebulæ having the special forms just referred to have been separated into stars; and that the gaseous spectrum has been found given, not only by quite a large number of isolated stars in the Swan, Argo, and elsewhere, but also by some nebulæ which have been resolved by the telescope.

Out of ten nebulæ given by the Earl of Rosse as certainly or probably resolvable, six give gaseous spectra. So that all the gaseous nebulæ, so called, may be composed of separate stars, may even be composed of stars like our sun, thinks Prof. Stone, Her Majesty's astronomer at the Cape of Good Hope. For such stars, at certain distances from us, and with certain relations as to thickness, heat, and density between their gaseous envelopes and their comparatively solid nuclei, would not be likely to report the nuclei in their spectra.

Further, it is claimed that continuous fire-mists would not be visible at such a vast remove from us and at such low temperatures as the nebulæ with gaseous spectra evidently are; that such mists could not have such permanent, irregular configurations, external and internal, and even vacant centres, as we sometimes notice; that such mists would never appear sharply defined and uniformly bright throughout as do many of the nebulæ in question; also, that such mists, if real, are not such in number, size, specimen stages, and chemical constitution as one would have a right to expect in what express the origin and end of all the stellar systems. Special stress is laid on the fact that in general not more than three elements, and sometimes less, are found in gaseous nebular spectra—viz., hydrogen, nitrogen, and one other element—whereas we ought to find as large a variety as compose the stars with their wealthy inventory.

As says Huggins, the eminent English spectroscopist, "The uniformity and extreme simplicity of the spectra of all the nebulæ oppose the opinion that this gaseous matter represents a nebulous fluid out of which the stars are elaborated. In such a primordial fluid all the elements entering into the composition of stars should be found. If these existed in these nebulæ the spectra of their light would be as crowded with bright lines as the stellar spectra are with dark lines."

These considerations will be found more fully stated in my work on "Evolution." They seem to me of great weight. We can hardly do less than say that, especially in the present state of spectrum analysis which allows such wide differences among experts and leaves largely uncertain the extent to which the spectrum of a given substance may be varied by numerous conditions, there is nothing to prevent our regarding all the nebulæ as so many Milky Ways, and saying with Sir John Herschel, "By far the greater part, probably at least nine-tenths, of the nebulous contents of the heavens consists of nebulæ of spherical or elliptical forms, presenting every variety of elongation and central condensation. Of these a great number have been resolved into distinct stars (by the reflector of the Earl of Rosse), and a vast multitude more have been found to present that mottled appearance which renders it almost a matter of certainty that an increase of optical power would show them to be similarly composed. A not unfair or unnatural deduction would therefore seem to be that those which resist such resolution do so only in consequence of the smallness and closeness of the stars of which they consist; that, in short, they are only optically and not physically nebulous. Although nebulæ do exist which even in this powerful telescope appear as nebulæ, without any sign of resolution, it may very reasonably be doubted whether there be really any essential distinction between nebulæ and clusters of stars."

IX. MOTIONS.

1. APPARENT.
2. REAL.
3. UNIVERSAL.
4. CUMULATIVE.
5. MIGHTY.
6. PRETEREA NIHIL.

IX. MOTIONS.

CERTAIN apparent motions of celestial objects must have been noticed from the beginning. Such is the daily motion from east to west that is common to them all, and by which their positions relative to one another are not disturbed in the least. A little closer observation next showed, and that at a time immemorially distant, that the sun, moon, and planets were constantly changing their places in respect to one another and the other celestial objects, and that each had its own law of change. And, until quite modern times, it was supposed that all these apparent motions were real, that all the heavenly bodies actually went around the earth once in 24 hours, and that, in addition to this common motion, a few were moving each on its own account. All the other heavenly bodies were supposed to have no motion at all among themselves, and so were called *fixed stars*.

A part of these views we have found incorrect; for example, the view that all the heavens go completely around the earth once a day. Had the ancients known how vast the heavens are, and at what vast distances from us many of its objects are placed, they would not have entertained such an idea for a moment. Think at what rate Capella, large as 430 suns like ours, would have to move in order, at a distance from us of more than 4,000,000 sun-distances to get around the earth in a day! Only about 14,000,-000,000 miles a second! Then think of all the stars, in their vast variety of distance from us, having their motions so adjusted to one another as to all make the circuit of the earth in exactly the same time! So we have to conclude that these apparent motions are not real, but are due to a revolution of the earth on itself from west to east, thus making all the contents of the sky appear to move from east to west. But this means a motion at our equator of 1,000 miles an hour.

Also, the apparent circuit of the sun among the stars is found not to be real, but to be produced by a revolution of the earth about the sun. Nothing but the supposition of such a revolution for the earth, and a similar one for each of the planets and comets, will reasonably explain the apparent motions of these various bodies. This will do it perfectly, if we only suppose the paths to be of a certain sort and moved in according to the law of gravity. But this, considering distances from the sun means for us another motion of 68,000 miles an hour, and for the planet Mercury one of 109,000, and for a certain comet at its fastest one of 1,200,000—velocities of altogether a different order from any that *we* can impress on matter, and in comparison with which the movements of our steam-cars and cannon balls are almost absurdly trifling. And whatever achievements in travelling the future may have in store for us as the fruits of mingled genius and science, we may be sure that none of them can ever give us anything like those sublime speeds which from time immemorial have been going on so easily and quietly in the silent heavens.

But it takes something more than the supposition of its motion about the sun to explain the aspects and apparent motions of the moon. We have to suppose, in addition, that it makes a complete circuit both about the earth and about one of its own diameters in every 27 days. This explains the observed fact that the same side of the moon is always presented to us. This also explains both phases and eclipses. In its course about the earth the moon sometimes passes through the earth's shadow and thus causes lunar eclipses; sometimes passes between us and the sun, and thus causes solar eclipses. But a monthly revolution about the earth at a distance from it of near 240,000 miles means an average motion of 54,000 miles an hour.

But the *sun itself*, is that the quiet, motionless centre of all these motions? "This cannot be," says the law of gravity. "The attractions between it and the bodies circulating about it require it to move about the common centre of gravity of all." And observation has detected still another motion of the sun. The stars in one part of the sky appear to be gradually separating from each other as by a common movement, while in the opposite quarter they are by a similar movement drawing together. This common movement is accounted for by supposing that the sun, with all the bodies belonging to it, is moving towards the constellation Hercules and away from the constellation Virgo. The rate of change in the apparent relative position of the stars we are approaching shows the rate of our motion—about 14,000 miles an hour.

But what of the fixed stars, so called? Are they really *fixed?* Being, as we have seen, masses of matter, the law of gravity requires them all to be in motion, even as our sun is. As we have seen, they are worlds on fire, vast fervid furnaces by which the great palace of nature is warmed and lighted, and so have motion within themselves of the most vehement and tumultuous sort. That each has also motion on an axis, as well as around the common centre of gravity of its planetary cortége, is inferable from what we know of our own system and the principle of gravity, as is also a translatory motion by which it and all its dependent worlds are borne away towards still ulterior centres of attraction. Actual observation has proved this last motion of so many stars that we feel sure that it belongs to all. Multitudes of stars are found undergoing minute changes of apparent place other than the common motion just mentioned. Star goes about star. Groups of stars move among themselves as if physically related. Some 700 are found moving on curve lines; while others, not visibly connected with any group or star, are seen stretching away towards unknown goals on apparently straight lines. By means of the displacement in the lines of their spectra, as already explained, Huggins has found that the following stars are approaching us or receding from us at a rate which cannot be explained by our own motion alone:

Approaching.

Deneb	39	miles per second.
Alpha Ursæ Majoris	46	"
Pollux	49	"
Vega	50	"
Arcturus	55	"

	Receding.
Rigel	15 miles per second.
Regulus	15 " "
Sirius	20 " "
Betelgeuse	22 " "
Castor	25 " "

Besides these motions in the line of vision there are others at right angles to that line of which our armored telescopes take note—multitudes of them. By taking account of their distance and annual angular movement, we find that some of yonder gold-and-silver-hooped cavalry are charging across the universe with enormous speed. Thus the star known as 1830 Groombridge, which at the distance of forty years from us, as light goes, moves annually over seven seconds of arc, must be moving at not far from 720,000 miles an hour—this on the supposition that the motion is all perpendicular to our axis of sight. Of course the actual motion is probably much greater than stated. Suppose we could stand off in space and see the huge, flaming system which this last star represents approaching us with its hundreds of worlds, and then sweeping sublimely and *closely* by at the rate of a million of miles an hour! We probably should get as near a just sense of almighty power as our faculties allow.

Everything on the earth is in movement. The atmosphere and waters, with their incessant and endless tides and currents, struggling ever towards an equilibrium which they never reach; the solid surface disintegrated by various elemental action and by the processes of vegetable and animal life, as well as shaken always and everywhere from below by struggling fires and gases into earthquakes, elevations, subsidences—really what earthly thing is at rest? What with the chemical, mechanical, physiological, and voluntary processes, there is not a single atom of the earth, however bound down and anchored it may seem, that is not moving among its fellow-atoms of the sphere. And then, as we have seen, the whole earth as one mass has at least four other great motions, viz., one on an axis, another as this axis describes a wavy line about the pole of the ecliptic, still another about the sun, and another still as it follows the sun across the universe towards Hercules. Each of these motions is absolutely continuous, without break for a single moment, and has been for—who shall say how long? And yet most of these motions, especially the mightiest of them, are as silent as the grave. Not the sharpest ear has ever caught the least sound, not the most sensitive nerve has felt the least jar, as the great world has gone on spinning and wheeling and rushing through the spaces and millenniums.

So it seems to be everywhere through the sky. We have fullest reason for saying that there is not an object in all yon populous and roomy heavens that is not subject to as great a variety of motions as besets all earthly things. Probably not a star, not an atom, is occupying at this moment a place it ever occupied before or will ever occupy again. And, as we have seen, the motion is often enormous. Many a Pegasus, instead of one, is coursing across the sky as if shod with light. Many an Argo, instead of one, is sailing across the blue deeps as if driven by all the winds that blow. And the movement of yonder pageant fleets and armies is as incessant as the flux of time. They are always campaigning. They never go into winter-quarters, nor even bivouac. Constant activity is to them the condition of safety. Is not the problem of the "perpetual motion" at last solved? Or is nature merely a machine acted on by forces from without?

Some will have it that there is hardly anything else in the universe besides motion. "Matter," say they, "has no other properties. Its heat, light, gravity, chemical affinities, sweetness or sourness, hardness, softness, color, weight, attractions, repulsions, life, thought, feelings, forces of all sorts, are merely varieties of one thing, viz, *motion.*" This is rather too startling a simplification of nature to get prompt acceptance from people who have a weakness for evidence, and would like to retain, if possible, some little foundation for religion. We object to the apotheosis of motion and the dethronement of God. We object to having, not only God, but even all nature itself, devoured by this modern divinity. This sort of Saturn will not give us a Golden Age. What assurance have we that the insatiable monster, after having devoured all things else, including his own children, will not at last proceed to devour himself and replace this magnificent universe by a tremendous Zero?

No, we reject motion as a divinity and as a universe. But we accept it as a *fact*, and a very great fact, especially in the astronomical realms. The whole vault is alive with it. Where the naked eye, however searching its gaze, never could find anything but absolute fixedness, persistent watching and measuring with superb instruments have found minute changes of place which, when uncoiled and interpreted in the light of the distance, show almost interminable stretches of space. We wonder to see the conjurer draw out of his sleeve or mouth endless lengths of ribbon—endless somethings apparently from merest nothings; but our mathematics is a still more wonderful conjurer, for, out of the merest fluxions of displacement which close telescopic observation detects among the stars, it draws almost unspeakable lengths of distance and motion.

X. ORBITS.

1. REALITY.
2. SHAPE.
3. INCLINATION
4. DIRECTION.
5. SIZE.

X. ORBITS.

It has incidentally been seen that the motion of some of the heavenly bodies is not on a straight line, but on a curve that practically returns into itself. The motions and aspects of the moon find their simplest explanation in the idea that it moves about the earth on what is nearly the circumference of a circle. The apparent motions of the sun and planets and most comets, as well as of the August and November meteoric clouds, are most reasonably accounted for by the supposition that these bodies, together with the earth, move about the sun in orbits which differ much among themselves as to shape and position.

The paths of the principal planets are nearly circular, and lie not far from the plane of the sun's rotation, and they are also traversed in the same direction in which the sun revolves. But among the asteroids and comets and meteor-clouds are found most striking exceptions in all these respects. The August meteors move in an orbit that touches our own, and yet goes out far beyond Neptune; and the orbit stands almost perpendicular to the solar equator. A very eccentric orbit also belongs to the November meteors, and their motion in it is retrograde. As much may be said of many comets. The satellites of Uranus also move from east to west in orbits nearly at right angles to the ecliptic. Such facts seem very significant. How can a rotation from west to east throw off a body from east to west? How can a rotation in a certain plane leave behind a body moving at right angles to that plane? How can a zone with a circular motion gather into a body with a motion almost parabolic? But, say some, "The eccentric comets are foreigners. They were generated outside of the solar system, and have been captured by the sun in its progress through space." It seems a sufficient answer to this that a comet must have always remained attached to the system from which it sprang, unless drawn off by the near approach of a stronger system, and that all the evidence we have on the matter is to the effect that the different celestial systems never approach within an almost immeasurable distance of one another.'

We also find that the motions of many of the "fixed stars" are orbital. Observation has shown this of some of the double stars, which under our own eyes have completed entire revolutions. But the orbit of a celestial body does not need to be completed before we can determine it to be an orbit. Every regular curve has its law of curvature which is deducible from a very small specimen arc. This arc is expressed by what are called the *elements* of the orbit, which may be determined often by a few observations. Of course, the greater the number of observations and the larger the arc dealt with, the greater will be the accuracy of the results. In the case of hundreds of double stars we have been able to see that their paths return into themselves; and in the case of some we have been able to determine the exact shape and size of the orbit. Others still are moving on what as yet seem straight lines; but this would be the seeming if the orbits were very large and the arcs as yet traversed under observation very small. And when we consider that the orbital path is universal among the celestial bodies nearest to us, and, indeed, among all whose paths have come sufficiently under our observation to allow us to judge conclusively the nature of their curve; and still more when we consider what the law of gravity requires for bodies moving obliquely towards one another in permanently friendly neighborhood, we easily satisfy ourselves that all the stars not only move, but move on curves that are orbits. But orbits cannot be parabolic or hyperbolic; they must be circular or elliptical. As a matter of fact they are, in general, *very* elliptical, very like the paths of comets. In two cases, those of Alpha Centauri and Gamma Virginis, the orbit is nearly five times longer than it is broad; and generally the length exceeds the breadth by more than a quarter of itself. This fact is a very significant one in its bearing on the nebular hypothesis.

Equally significant in the same direction is the fact that in some multiple stars the planes of revolution are largely inclined to one another, while they are not known to be coincident, or nearly so, in a single instance. The general telescopic aspect of some groups and clusters tells the same story of them; for they are so densely crowded towards the centre, and are otherwise so characterized, as to force on us the idea of stars arranged in globular or other solid forms. The great cluster in Hercules, another in Libra, and still another known as 30 Doradûs, are examples. Of course, in a globular cluster the orbits about a common centre must have to one another every degree of inclination. How can this be reconciled with the notion that the worlds in the same neighborhood have all sprung from one central rotation?

Let Sir John Herschel answer in words that cover a much broader question: "If the theory be regarded as receiving the smallest support from any observed numerical relations which actually hold good among the elements of the planetary orbits, I beg leave to demur. Assuredly it receives no support from the observation of the effect of sidereal aggregation as exemplified in the formation of globular and elliptic clusters. For we see this cause, working out in thousands of instances, to have resulted not in the formation of a single large central body surrounded by a few smaller attendants disposed in one plane around it, but in systems of infinitely greater complexity, consisting of multitudes of nearly equal luminaries grouped together in solid globular or elliptic forms."

Among the celestial ellipses we know of none less than that which Neptune describes about the sun, that is one 18,000,000,000 of miles in sweep. The distance between two mutually revolving stars cannot be greater than the diameter of one orbit and may be only about one-half of it. As the distance between the two suns of Alpha Centauri is about the distance of Neptune from our sun, one of the two component stars cannot have a less orbit than that planet. As the distance between the two suns of 61 Cygni is about three times the sun-distance of Neptune, one of the companions must have at least a sweep three times that of Neptune. As the distance between Mizar and Alcor in the tail of the Great Bear is about

360 times the sun-distance of Neptune, one of those twin stars must have at least a path that would cover that of the planet 360 times. As the distance between our sun and Alcyone is about 300,000 Neptunian sun-distances, that great number expresses the number of times the greatest planetary orbit of our solar system would have to be applied to the other in order to measure out all its prodigious length. But then it is generally thought that our sun is comparatively near the heart of that great neighborhood of suns that we call the Milky Way; and if this is so, what a trifle even this last orbit must be compared with that described by one of our frontier suns! Why, that frontier sun, according to the soundings of Sir William Herschel, is 500 years of light-travel away from us, i. e., more than 6,000,000 Neptunian sun-distances. And then the still grander sweep of Milky Way about Milky Way, of nebula about nebula! Ah, what a cosmos is included in that last stupendous curve! Were a sun to flash along it, leaving behind a permanent wake of glory, generations after generations of men would pass away before that glorious wake would come to differ sensibly from a straight line to human eye or instrument. When one comes to fairly think of it, the expanse included within the path of the humblest planet is some-

thing fearful. But when one sees a sun putting its fiery girdle about an entire Milky Way with its 18,000,000 of sun-orbits, nay, about a great host of itinerant Milky Ways, and wheeling through the trackless and benighted spaces as if pursued by Omnipotence and yet doing it as accurately and safely as if guided by steel tramways, our hearts almost forget to beat. It is akin to the sublimity of God.

XI. PERIODS.

1. OF ROTATION.
2. OF REVOLUTION.
3. AS RELATED.
4. AS VARIOUS.
5. AS VAST.
6. AS CONSTANT.

XI. PERIODS.

The sun and all planets and satellites whose circumstances are such as to allow of *rotations* being observed if they actually exist, are found to have them—varying in length of period from about ten hours, in the cases of Jupiter and Saturn, to twenty-seven days, as in the case of our moon. That all the worlds of space rotate cannot be proved from any known law or force requiring rotation; and yet, I suppose, astronomers, almost to a man, would expect to find rotation in every celestial body, as well as a general spherical form, could it be subjected to a close examination. And they would also expect to find the time of rotation stable in every case, just as it appears to be everywhere in the solar system. The length of our day has not sensibly changed during the historic period. No other rotations have been found to change in the least. Each is not only uniform in its rate from moment to moment, but it is completed from age to age in exactly the same time. There is indeed a speculation that in the case of the earth there are disturbing causes at work tending to retard its rotation and to bring the times of rotation and revolution together. We are told of the friction of the tides and tradewinds. We are told the planets rotate in a resisting medium. We are told that if one side of a planet, from any cause, becomes loaded or weightier than another, the attractions on it from without would no longer be as if all its matter were condensed at its centre, and so a disturbance of the rotation must result. Still the great fact remains that no such disturbance has been detected by the most careful and skilled observation. Are we to infer that the change which has really taken place is so minute that it has not had time to accumulate into observation in 2,000 years, or that, though considerable, it is cancelled by a system of compensations such as is found largely in nature; or is the earth a well-balanced, symmetrically-weighted orb, revolving in a vacuum, and incapable of being cosmically disturbed by the agitations within itself? For aught that yet appears the celestial rotation-periods are absolutely constant.

As soon as we know the time in which the earth goes around the sun, and the mean distances of the planets from the same body, we know their periods of *revolution* by means of the law which Kepler found tentatively and which Newton proved from the law of gravitation, viz., *The squares of the periodic times of any two planets are to each other as are the cubes of their mean distances from the sun.* Another law detected by the same great observer and mathematically deduced by the same great geometer, viz., *The radius-vector of a revolving body* (that is, the straight line joining it to its primary) *describes equal areas in equal times*, also enables us to calculate the time of a complete revolution by observing how long it takes that line to traverse a given small area. Thus we have been able to get the periods of revolution of many bodies in all parts of the heavens: e. g.

Mercury .	88 days,	Uranus	. 84 years,	
Venus	. 225 "	Neptune	. 165 "	
Mars . .	2 years,	Comet of 1858,		2,100
Jupiter .	12 "	"	1811,	3,000
Saturn .	29 "	"	1844,	100,000

Comte undertook to show that the period of revolution of any planet is just the period of rotation which the sun must have had when filling its orbit. As to his success, the younger Herschel, as illustrious in physical astronomy as in practical, after pointing out certain omissions and assumptions which really postulated the point to be proved, expresses himself thus: "Where, I would ask, is there a student to be found, who has graduated as a senior optime in this university, who will not at once lay his finger on the fallacy of such an argument and pronounce it a vicious circle?" And M. Babinet, a distinguished member of the French Academy of Sciences, proceeded to show by mathematics that were not "circular" that the rotation period of the supposed solar nebula at the distance of the earth must have been more than 3,000 years, and at the distance of Neptune nearly 3,000,000 years, "numbers," he says, "so infinitely superior to those which mark the times of revolution of the earth and Neptune that it is impossible to admit that these bodies have been formed from the mass of the sun expanded to the planetary orbits."

It has already been noticed that the inner moon of Mars goes about that planet more than three times during one of its rotations. But at the time when the Martial nebula extended as far as the satellite its rotation would have been considerably slower still. This fact is probably the severest blow the nebular hypothesis has yet received from within the solar system. Says an American astronomer, "To reconcile its motion with any conceivable theory of the genesis (natural) of the solar system, it is almost necessary to suppose that Phobos is not where it was made, or else that the planet has had its time of rotation changed." Of course such suppositions, without the least color of verisimilitude from any fact, are inadmissible in the courts of science.

For periods outside of our system see the following table:

Zeta Herculis	36 years.
Zeta Cancri	60 "
Alpha Centauri	75 "
Omega Leonis	82 "
Gamma Coronæ Borealis	100 "
Delta Cygni	178 "
Beta Cygni	500 "
Gamma Leonis	1,200 "
Mizar	200,000 "
Quadruple star near Vega	
One pair	4,000 "
Another pair	12,000 "
Pair about pair	1,000,000 "
Our sun about Alcyone	20,000,000 "
Frontier star " "	100,000,000 "

We see that the time of revolution is wonderfully different for different bodies. One of the Martial moons goes about its primary in about seven hours. The comet of 1844 goes about the sun in 100,000 years. Among the fixed stars we find a like difference. The 700 composite stars in which an orbital motion has been observed have periods varying from 36 years in the case of

Zeta Herculis, to 1,200 years in the case of Gamma Leonis, and 200,000 in the case of Mizar, and a million in the case of the quadruple star near Vega. See something even grander than this, viz., the 20 millions of years in which our sun circumnavigates Alcyone or some other centre. See something grander still: the 100 millions of years in which the outmost star of the Milky Way wheels about the whole great nebulæ. And there is something still grander among the nebulæ.

These periods of revolution, like those of rotation, are grandly constant. The length of our year remains steadfastly the same. So does our lunar month, or period of the moon's revolution about the earth. So does each planetary year, or time of revolution about the sun. When we have once found the year of Neptune to be 165 of our years we can count on these figures as good for all time. Wherever we find the planet in its orbit to-day, there our successors will find it at the end of each 165 years for thousands of years to come. So everywhere among the periods. Constancy reigns. Our astronomical lists just given will not need revision as the years roll on. Whatever slight changes occur have fixed periods of oscillation, and the average periodic time remains steadfastly the same. One thinks of Him who is "the same yesterday and to-day and for ever."

See how abysses of space are matched by abysses of time! We have been lost in the endless stretches of distance and orbital sweep: now we are lost in almost endless stretches of duration. How puny our lives on this planet seem in the presence of these little eternities that we are ever falling in with among the starry Methuselahs! They help our limping thought towards a conception of our own immortality and of the Eternal One. Evidently He who laid out his scheme of worlds on such a stupendous scale of time as well as of space has a plenty of time at his disposal, is not hemmed in by the narrow chronologies of human history, can afford to count a thousand years as one day. He has the freedom of inexhaustible oceans of duration from which to draw. Our astronomy here shows us another ladder whose successive rounds of ever-widening periods gradually strain our ascending thought towards some faint and awe-inspiring conception of Him who inhabiteth eternity.

XII. PERTURBATIONS.

1. A SUPPOSITION.
2. GENERAL PROBLEM.
3. PARTIAL ANSWERS.
4. PERIODIC VARIATIONS.
5. CERTAIN USES.

XII. PERTURBATIONS.

THE orbits which the heavenly bodies describe, when narrowly looked into, are found to be more or less disturbed by their mutual actions. The earth is not only attracted by the sun, but also by all the other members of the solar system. If the sun were the sole attracting body, our planet would describe an accurate and permanent ellipse about their common centre of gravity. As it is, with so many attracting neighbors, the path which we actually take through space is more or less *disturbed*, or made wavy in every direction. Astronomers take account of these deflections from the orbit which the earth would traverse if not disturbed, by supposing the orbit itself to be acted on instead of the earth—to be elongated, tilted this way and that, made to revolve in its own plane—thus made to accompany the earth in all its movements. These supposed changes in the form and position of the orbit, made to accommodate the shifting course of the planet, are called its *perturbations*. As each member of the solar system, great or small, with ever-varying distance and direction from us, has something to do with creating these perturbations, to estimate their amount so as to find the actual place of the earth at any moment is a difficult matter. Indeed, it cannot be done with absolute accuracy by any science yet known to us.

But even this problem is not as difficult as that which actually presents itself. For actually the earth is subject not only to the attractions of the other members of the solar system, but to those of all the other bodies in space. None but the Creator could take exact account of all these. Happily, perfect exactness is not needed by us. The influence of the sun is so immensely preponderant that it is only important to consider a few of the larger perturbations by other bodies, and to make only approximate estimates for them. And yet we must not forget that an infinite number of other disturbances exist, which, for aught our science can show, may, in the course of the great future, bring about very great results.

What is true of our earth is true of every other celestial body away to the outskirts of nature. Its path is bent hither and thither in every possible direction by the innumerable attractions of all other bodies. And each of these other bodies is continually changing its direction and distance. Hence to determine with perfect precision any given celestial path is quite beyond all human faculty. The problem belongs only to an Infinite mind. Much more does it belong only to an Infinite mind to give the exact place at any one moment of all the revolving orbs that rush and shine through the immensities. What a tangled wilderness of attractions! What a misty abyss of interactions! Each perturbation has superimposed on itself an infinity of other perturbations, and each of these others carries a like infinite series, and so on indefinitely. The resultant of this complex of forces, could anything be more beyond the reach of human calculus? But there is One who knows it perfectly. The intuitions of God put to shame the logic of differentials and integrals. The problem of the perturbations, in all its wondrous breadth, is simplicity itself to his gaze. He is the only real astronomer. When I think how long it was before even the most gifted men reached a passable solution of the problem of two revolving bodies, and of how few they are who can even comprehend an explanation of this most elementary solution, this first term of an infinite series whose terms advance by a factor which is at once complex, variable, and infinite, and then think of the dimensions and bewildering intricacy of this stupendous thicket of universal attraction with its curves within curves, web interlaced with web, "in endless mazes lost," and yet seen through at a glance by that all-devouring Intelligence which first devised great nature and ever since has kept open eye on the exact whereabout of every orb in all in its dense fog of labyrinthian interactions and wanderings, then it is that I profoundly realize the difference between man and God.

Though the complete problem of the perturbations is so wonderfully beyond us, yet we have found out some very interesting things about them. One of these is that the perturbations of the solar system, considered apart from external bodies, are all of them periodic, alternately increasing and diminishing within certain fixed limits. This on the supposition that the mass of the central body is much greater than all the other bodies together; that the orbits are nearly circular, nearly in the same plane and traversed in the same direction—a supposition that substantially agrees with fact, as they are only comets, asteroids, and satellites whose orbits and directions do not conform to this requirement. The masses of these bodies are so small that it is generally conceded that their non-conformity will not affect the periodical character of the perturbations. Nor probably would the existence of an extremely attenuated medium in the interplanetary spaces, such as has been supposed essential to light. But this medium is as yet mere conjecture.

The perturbations in the solar system have

periods of exceeding variety in many respects, especially as to length. Some make their round in a few years, while others consume many ages, and so are called secular. Thus the perturbation of the earth's axis known as the Nutation has a period of about 19 years, while that called the Precession of the Equinoxes has a period of 26,000. In some cases we have still larger figures, mounting into the millions.

By means of the perturbations the Calculus has come to great improvements. The endeavor to find out their causes and amounts has almost re-created our higher mathematics. The old principles and methods which Newton used so mightily needed to be developed and reinforced by new discoveries before they could grapple successfully with anything more than the simpler forms of perturbation. So vast pains were taken to perfect the instrument of investigation. Under the labors of such men as Clairaut, Laplace, and Lagrange it became able to explain and estimate with sufficient precision all the important disturbances of the solar system—in fact, has become the most wonderful instrument of scientific discovery the world has ever known. The brawn of the giant was largely gained by wrestling with the perturbations. It is the old story—struggle and strength. As struggling with winds and winters has made the great oak what it is, as struggling with the difficult builds up both body and mind of the youth into a forceful and executive manhood, so struggling with these stubborn perturbations has gradually built up the infant Calculus of Newton and Leibnitz into a glorious maturity.

Also by means of the perturbations we have been able to discover one planet, Neptune, and not improbably will be able to discover others—say, if you please, Intra-Mercurial or Extra-Neptunian. When we find a disturbance in the orbit of a body which its known neighbors will not account for we are entitled to say, as was said in the case of Uranus, "There is some other body in the neighborhood whose mass and orbit are such as to cause the trouble."

Also, as the amount of trouble at any given point depends solely on the mass, distance, and direction of the troubling neighbor, if the last two elements are known we are able to find the mass concerned in a given perturbation. In this way the masses of the planets that have no satellites, and also of the satellites themselves, have been determined. In the case of such planets as have satellites their masses can be inferred from the curvature of the orbits of the satellites at any point; for if we know the tangential velocity of a satellite at any point the amount of deflection from a tangent in a given time measures the attractive force of the primary, and so its quantity of matter. This deflection from a tangent is itself really a perturbation—a disturbance of the rectilinear motion which but for it would be permanent. When the masses of the sun and planets are known we readily find their mean densities, their sizes being given. In the following list these elements are given for the leading members of the solar system, the mass and density of the earth being taken as units:

	Mass.	Density.
Mercury	.065	1.24
Venus	.785	.92
Earth	1.000	1.00
Mars	.124	.92
Jupiter	300.857	.22
Saturn	90.032	.12
Uranus	12.641	.18
Neptune	16.761	.17
Sun	354,000.000	.25

We should expect that, were the planets generated naturally from a nebulous mass, the sun would be the densest body in the system, and the planets would decrease regularly in density to the outskirts. But actually the sun is among the least dense bodies; Mars is equal to Venus, which is inferior to the earth; while Saturn is inferior to Uranus.

Of course the same method is theoretically applicable for determining the masses and densities of many stars. If the orbit which one star describes about another can be so known that its exact law of curvature at any given point can be found, we are able to find at that point the proportion between the centrifugal and centripetal forces on which alone the curvature depends. But the centrifugal force is virtually given in the direction and velocity at that point; and the latter element is given by the known period and orbital place in connection with Kepler's law that a radius-vector must describe equal areas in equal times. But as we can know what effect our sun would produce at the same distance, we have the means of comparing the masses of the central star and our sun. The only difficulty is in determining with sufficient precision the elements of such remote orbits.

XIII. SYSTEMS.

1. APPARENT DISORDER.
2. SUPPOSED ORGANIZATIONS.
3. THE REAL.
4. NOTABLE FEATURES.

XIII. SYSTEMS.

No star is a hermit. Though individualized in the heavens as islands are in the ocean, though separated from one another by what seem endless spaces, all the heavenly bodies are in a state of organized society. They compose great and orderly communities. They hang together, by no means loosely; they act on one another constantly and powerfully; they interchange various good offices; they move harmoniously with reference to one another; they obey common laws and have common pivots of revolution; no force ever succeeds in breaking the mighty though invisible bonds that unite them. Call them families, clans, tribes, armies, nations — nations, as we shall see, with no civil wars or real dissensions among them, no changes of constitution or government or dynasty or even by-laws.

And yet the heavenly bodies have not an artificial arrangement that at once strikes the eye and suggests a manufactured article, as Sir John Herschel said the elements of matter did to him. On the contrary, at a first view the stars seem sown at haphazard through the void; it is a kingdom of pell-mell and disorder that we see, a vast mob of everlasting fireflies pinned to the vault. But this view has never been satisfactory to thoughtful people. The scientific instinct has felt that, beneath the surface, there must be a principle of orderly arrangement, and has from time immemorial been conjecturing what that principle may be. Are not the heavens built about the earth in a series of concentric crystal spheres, each having its own peculiar law of motion, but all moved by the outermost sphere of all, a *primum mobile?* This original supposition became complicated by other suppositions as new facts gradually came into view and demanded explanation, until the full Ptolemaic system, with its outfits of cycles, deferents, epicycles, held unchallenged possession of the scholarly world, and continued to hold, century after century. But such a system did not satisfy Tycho Brahé. Instead of granting that the whole heavens move about the earth directly, he maintained that the planets move primarily about the sun and then with the sun about the earth. This idea was better, but not best. A little later Copernicus revived the theory of Pythagoras, for long ages completely dead and buried, that the sun is the centre of revolution, not only of the planets, but of the earth itself. At last we have the beginning of the true system of the heavens. The Copernican system is demonstrably true; its predecessors are demonstrably false. This is rational; the others, to our present knowledge, are ridiculous.

But as yet we have only a glimpse at the true system of the heavens. We see only a planet with a moon or moons revolving about it, and then a number of planets with their moons revolving about the sun. But how about the innumerable remainder of celestial worlds? We have elsewhere shown that these are gathered into still higher and grander systems of revolution. In addition to satellite and planetary systems we can make out sun systems, group systems, cluster systems, nebula systems, ulterior systems, an ultimate or universe system.

Consider the heavens as one vast neighborhood. According to the law of gravity, all this grand total of stars must revolve about their common centre of gravity. This is the *ultimate system*. But this ultimate neighborhood is distributed into great sub-neighborhoods, each of two or more nebulæ (see examples about the poles of the Milky Way), each neighborhood widely separated from its fellows, and therefore revolving about its own centre of gravity. This is an *ulterior system*. Of nebulæ, each is widely apart from its fellows—a veritable island in space—and therefore must revolve about its own centre of gravity.

This is a *nebula system*. Each nebula consists of two or more clusters of stars, each cluster widely apart from its fellow-clusters, and therefore revolving about its own centre of gravity. This is a *cluster system*. Each cluster consists of two or more groups of stars, each group widely apart from its fellows, and therefore revolving about its own centre of gravity. This is a *group system*. Each group consists of two or more sets of suns, each set widely apart from its fellows, and therefore revolving about its own centre of gravity. This is a *sun system*. Each of the suns in a sun system has about it several planets, each sun family widely apart from its fellows, and therefore revolving about its own centre of gravity. This is a *planet system*. A planet generally has near it one or more satellites. This little family also is widely apart from similar ones, and therefore must revolve about its own centre of gravity. This is a *satellite system*, the elementary unit of celestial organization.

As we ascend from this simplest class of systems, the interval between systems of the same class continually widens, just as does the interval between varieties, between species, between genera, between orders or families, between classes in living organisms. What an organic interval between the vertebrate and radiate animals as

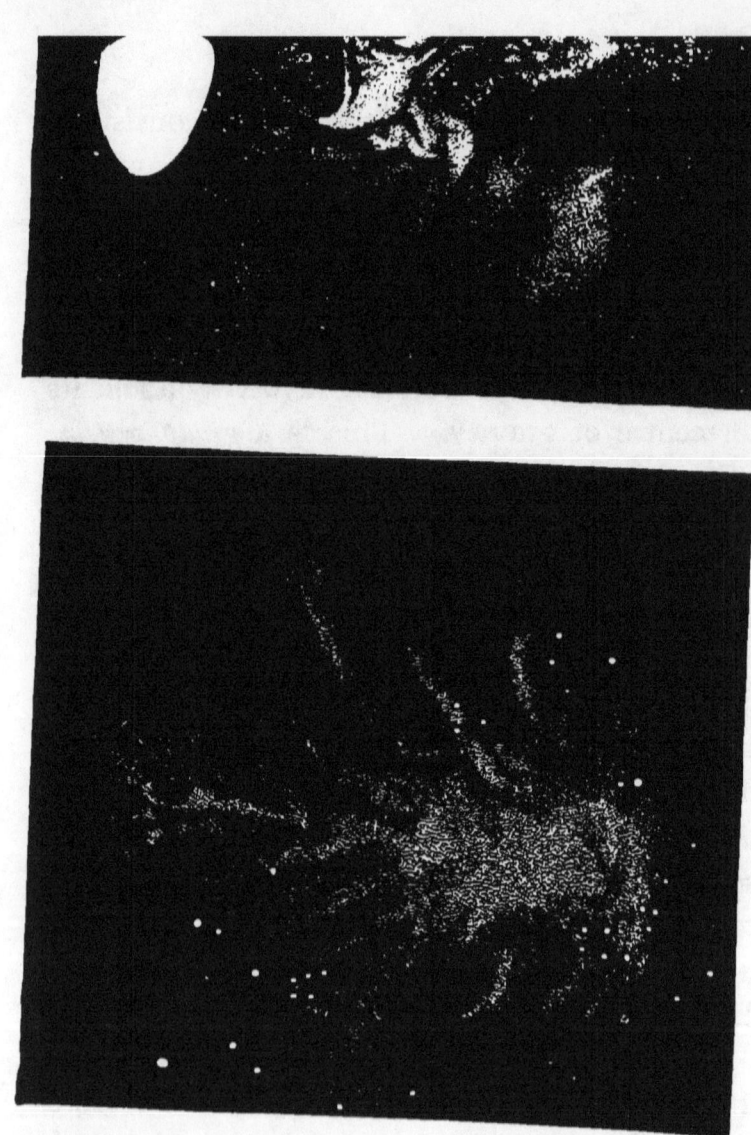

IRREGULAR NEBULÆ: IN TAURUS AND IN ORION. SEE PAGE 101.

compared with that between different varieties of pigeons or of men! What a space-interval between nebulæ as compared with that between satellite systems! It seems as if the Builder was far more concerned to prevent the possibility of the mutual interference of the greater systems than of the smaller, as he might well be.

Such are some of the celestial systems. Doubtless they are very far from being all. Between the satellite system and the universe system there may be an almost infinite number of distinct neighborhoods and centres of revolution; and our moon may be coursing at one and the same time not only about the earth and about the sun and about Alcyone, but about millions of other centres, while wheeling out that greatest curve of all which is to go about the heart of all creation. Will it ever be able to complete such an ellipse as that? Will it last long enough to finish such a journey? And is it purely by forces inherent in mere earthy matter that it goes steadily on from age to age, working out, without faltering and without confusion, its vast complex of orbits? As each system embraces satellite systems, each has an indefinite number of orbits, gradually ascending in grandeur and in the dignity of their centres, until at last we come to those that sweep around the common centre of gravity of the whole universe. Wheel within wheel, orbit taking hold on orbit in unimaginable spirals—what a tangled Black Forest of motions which no human genius, though yoked to superhuman industry, can ever find a way through!

All celestial systems are stupendous in their outspread with reference to any unit of magnitude used on the earth. But some among them quite confound us, and almost take our breath away by their stupendousness. Those cluster systems in Libra and Hercules, each of them has thousands of suns packed together into an intense and unspeakable glory within a space about one-tenth of that occupied by the moon, and yet without appreciable parallax. If the 30,000 suns, or more, which compose the Herculean system are only as far apart from one another as we are from the nearest fixed star, the diameter of the system must be formidable—almost to an angel's wing.

But look at a nebula system, the one best known to us, viz., the Milky Way. According to the soundings of Sir William Herschel, this system spreads its 18,000,000 of suns, with their planets and satellites, over a space whose diameter is not far from 180,000,000 diameters of the earth's orbit, or 1,000 years of light-travel.

If we look away from our Milky Way to other Milky Ways, we find them sometimes apparently related to each other, as are the double and multiple stars. Nay, we find large groups and even clusters of nebulæ of about the same brightness and general aspect, coming into view with about the same optical powers, evidently belonging to the same order of distances from us. In the Magellanic Clouds we have a cluster of 300 firmaments. In the wing of Virgo we have one of 1,000 firmaments. Just think of the space occupied and swept over by that last ulterior system! Suppose its members to average as large as the firmament to which we belong, though Sir William Herschel thought ours to be one of the smaller firmaments. This, as has been said, it takes light 1,000 years to cross. But we have good reason to believe that the interval between any two nebulæ is vastly greater than the breadth of one of them. What is the breadth of a satellite system compared with the average interval between satellite systems? — of planet systems or sun systems or group systems compared with the average intervals between those systems respectively? And, as we have seen, the disparity grows rapidly as we ascend in the scale of systems. Accordingly the intervals that separate the various members of that great firmament system in Virgo must be vastly greater than any we have yet considered, and the spaces occupied and traversed by that chiliad of travelling firmaments must be almost infinitely greater still. Millions of years of light-travel would be required for crossing it. The old Hermes would never have undertaken such a task. The most audacious imagination refuses to do it, unless it be crazed as well as audacious.

But what is even such a system compared with that final congeries of systems which includes all the orbs of space as they go wheeling sublimely about that innermost pivot of revolution which it is so easy to believe is the central throne of Deity as well as of gravity! No words of man can properly express such an accumulation of magnitudes. Our intelligence does not begin to master it. Even our imaginations lie dazed and helpless before such lengths and breadths. Space is absolutely infinite; and our telescopes, as they rise in space-penetrating power, are ever bringing into view new firmaments, and give us no hints whatever of nearing the frontiers of the stellar universe. Science from her last watch-tower lifts both hands in astonishment and despair. Then fancy, fresh and strong of wing, takes up the fallen measuring line and goes outward faster than the beams of light, and still outward, and outward still for ever so long among the unending suns, until she too at last grows faint of wing, and with pale and gasping lips invokes the angels. "O Michael, the prince, take thou this measuring-rod which I can hold no longer, and carry it to the last world that sweeps about the throne of the Eternal." And the angel shook his glorious wings and folded them again. "You ask of me the impossible. Strong as are my pinions, they are not equal to such a task as this. From this point outward I have often gone for never, never so long among the firmaments, and never yet have I reached the place where there did not seem as much of a glory of worlds before me as behind me. The last world—the *last* world! no, I cannot undertake to find that. You must go to Him who created it. All we angels have to say after we have taken our widest flights is, Lo, these are parts of His ways! How small a portion is known of Him; but the thunder of His power who can understand?"

XIV. STABILITIES.

1. UNSTABLE SYSTEMS.
2. LAGRANGE'S THEOREM.
3. STELLAR EQUILIBRIUM.
4. LOCAL CATASTROPHES.

XIV. STABILITIES.

Stars are no tramps, disorderly vagrants whose whereabouts for any length of time cannot be counted on. They are bound up together in systems over which law reigns.

But, then, systems under law are not always stable. They often decay in a short time. They not seldom come into mutual conflict, and shatter one another to pieces. Corporeal systems, social systems, political systems, systems of philosophy and religion—they have been known to meet one another like opposing battering-rams in full career; and, lo, the field is covered with ruins!

How is it with these shining systems above in their bewildering numbers and impetuous courses? Do they after a while fall to pieces of themselves? Are they mutually destructive? Do they impinge, collide, switch one another off into aimeless vagrancy and final wreck?

Lagrange has shown that if all the members of a planet system, both planets and satellites, revolve in a vacuum about a central body far greater in mass than all of them, in orbits nearly circular, nearly in the same plane, and traversed in the same direction, the system will be stable for ever, unless some force from without interferes to destroy it. But these conditions of stability do not all exist. There is reason to suspect that we are not moving in a void. And we know of several minor bodies of the system whose orbits are very eccentric, very much out of the general plane of the system, and traversed from east to west. To be sure the inter-planetary ether, if it exists, must be extremely attenuated: also the non-conformist comets, asteroids, and satellites are of small masses relatively; but who can assure us that these small elements of confusion, contradiction, and disorder may not after a long time so accumulate their effects as to subvert the system? No one has yet done this. It is certain, however, that our system is in a condition of stable equilibrium so far as *main* points of structure are concerned; and it may yet be proved that these main things are able to dominate and neutralize all the elements of instability—just as it has been proved that small deviations from the circular form or a common plane in orbits can be dominated, and just as the conservative forces in some great empire may be so immensely preponderant over the destructive as to put it quite out of danger from the petty misdemeanors of scattered individuals. As a matter of fact, the bodies of our system have been observed rolling harmoniously together for an immensely long period; we know of no instance of collision or precipitation into the sun by means of the mazy actions and counteractions of the rushing orbs with their ever-changing configuration and everlasting itineracy.

The same may be said of any other celestial system. During all the long time in which the sky has been observed, has any star been known to strike against any other star? Stars have been occulted often—that is, other bodies have passed tween us and them so as to hide them from view; but after a while they have appeared again quite unharmed. Stars have sometimes disappeared without sensible occultation, or have suddenly flamed up into unusual splendor; but never as the result of known collision with other bodies, and generally under circumstances inconsistent with it.

When we consider the vast number of moving worlds that lie under the gaze of our telescopes, the headlong speed and endless variety of direction with which they are moving, and the unspeakable complications involved in such a maelstrom of interdependent orbits, such chronic, not to say everlasting, freedom from mutual conflict and disaster is something wonderful. Individual men often interfere with one another; ships on the high seas come together and sink; families shock against families, parties against parties, nations against nations, on the fields of business, diplomacy, and battle; even religious denominations do not always manage to get along without mutual interference; I had almost said that interferences and conflicts with one another are not wholly unknown among the very scientists themselves, both satellites and primaries. And yet above us we see a shining empire where from time immemorial reigns unalterable concord—individuals, families, parties, nations, all packed with mighty forces and rushing with stormy energy in every conceivable direction, and yet, so far as we can see, always religiously respecting the safety and rights of one another. It looks very much like intelligent prearrangement. It looks very much like a current Providence. It is quite in harmony with the idea that at the heart of our astronomy there is a KING who knows how to govern into order and safety even a boundless empire.

Yes, the heavens are stable: "For that He is strong in power not one faileth." Still we would not like to say that the present celestial arrangements are unending. They have looked down in undecaying beauty and splendor on all past human generations, and, for aught we know, may look down in unbroken quiet on as many more. But at last a catastrophe will come—at least to the earth and its atmosphere. The heavens being on fire shall be dissolved, and the elements melt with fervent heat, and the earth and all things therein shall be burned up. That will befall our earth which seems to have occasionally befallen other celestial bodies. A new star suddenly flames out to view till it is visible at noonday, gradually decreases in brightness, and at last disappears permanently. Is not this the exit of a consumed world? However this may be, *our* fate is sure. But this does not necessarily mean a celestial collision. There are other means of setting a world on fire. Besides, the "sure word of prophecy" tells us that the event will be wholly unexpected by the men then living; which could not be if the disaster should result from the gradual approach of another world to ours. Men would see the approaching body ever increasing in size and splendor, till at last it would fill the whole sky. The warning of the coming disaster would be ample to all mankind; it would not come "as a snare" on men, "as the lightning," and find men "eating and drinking, marrying and giving in marriage."

XV. FORCES.

1. TERRESTRIAL.
2. CELESTIAL.
3. TOTAL.

XV. FORCES.

LET us listen! What is that we hear, like the far-off march of armies or the voices of distant seas or the rustle of infinite wings in the depths of heaven? The air is full of delicate noise—the seeds and ghosts of sound rather than sound itself—on the broad bosom of which come out occasionally in relief the notes of birds, the lowing of cattle, the sighing of winds, the murmur of brooks, the voices of men. What is it? It is the omnipresent voice of *change*.

Something is happening. Many things are happening. In fact, no end of things are happening with every indivisible moment. The earth and every particular thing it contains is in a state of constant flux. Each new instant a new deluge of change sweeps all round the globe. Not a nook is left unfilled, not a peak is left uncovered. There is at least one universal deluge. No one thing maintains for any appreciable time absolutely the same place, form, size, color, constitution, or appearance. Not one thing is to-day as it was yesterday, or even as it was a moment ago. It changes while we are looking at it, however briefly; nay, the looking eye itself has changed since the look began. Yonder animal, yonder tree, yonder stone, yonder anything, is ever in process of becoming something else. Wherever we look novelties are coming and going in infinite swarms. The most stable things we know of (to say nothing of the restless ocean and the still more restless atmosphere, and, if you please, the still more restless ether) are going and coming, increasing or diminishing, maturing or decaying, becoming brighter or darker, forsaking this shape for that, shading from one hue to another, passing out of this relation to its neighbors into a different. Everything is swept along by ten thousand different currents—swept down upon from the skies, swept up to from the depths, swept in upon from every point of the horizon. The past, the present, the future, all break against it in ceaseless waves. Change charges on us in armies upon armies. Every leaf trembles and throbs with transition. Every day is hasting towards night, and every night towards day. Every day is effervescing into to-morrow. What with spring, summer, autumn, winter, the face of the earth is a calculus of variations. "Up and away!" seems the motto for everything. Every molecule is circulating. Every atom is ever seeking equilibrium and never finding it. Ocean, atmosphere, and ether are hardly more restless than the solid land which is vibrating ceaselessly down to the very centre with the tramp and play and rage of teeming populations and nomadic elements. And *spirit*, with which in its different grades the earth is so immensely peopled, is even more mercurial than matter, more sensitive to influence than the very clouds and gases and ethers, more easily driven through all the moods and tenses of thought and feeling and volition than the vapors are into all shapes and places by strong winds. Now and then transition is abrupt and sonorous; but generally things glide quietly from one state to another in grave respect for the doctrine of continuity: the old is father to the new, and the new carries all the future in its womb.

And, doubtless, our changeful world is but a sample of all others. We have seen how full the astronomical heavens are of motions—how motion is crowded on motion, that is, change on change, in cycles and epicycles without end. Surely it is yonder as it is here. Change, unceasing change, universal change, change on a most wonderful and confounding scale, is the very condition of stability in all the regions accessible to our telescopes. As here, so everywhere and always through the blue immensities, are flying the shuttles of an infinite weaving and unweaving; new patterns are waxing and old ones are waning, and Penelope unmakes her web as fast as she makes it.

Now these changes, great and small, sensible and insensible, gradual and abrupt, that flood all nature are due to certain causes which we call forces. What the ultimate nature of these forces is it may not be easy to say; but it is easy to arrange them into classes according to the nature of the changes they cause. So we speak of mechanical forces, of chemical forces, of vital forces, of spiritual forces, and refer to each class its proper class of changes. Thus the changes of day and night we ascribe to the mechanical force, whatever it may be, that causes the rotation of the earth on its axis; the changes of the seasons to gravity and projectile force, carrying the earth about the sun with axis inclined to its plane of revolution; the changes expressed in the perturbations called the tides, the precession of the equinoxes, the nutation of the earth's axis, to gravity as exerted by the sun and moon. Thus the changes in the intimate composition and structure of bodies, as various elements unite or separate, are ascribed to an attractive force called chemical residing in each element and which differs from gravity in that it acts only at insensible distances and differs in degree towards different substances. Also, the changes that take place in living organisms, whether vegetable or animal, connected with circulation, nutrition, growth, reproduction, are referred ultimately to another class of forces called vital which somehow underlie and use the chemical and mechanical forces and are sufficiently different from them to deserve another name.

These different classes of forces are often supposed to be only different forms of one thing, and this one thing is supposed to be motion. Some say that this motion is the ultimate force, that it resides only in matter, that it is indestructible, eternal, and invariable in amount. Others, by the same general way of thinking, deny this, and say that all the modes of motion are purely the product of a personal divine force which is the real cause of every occurrence. Still others stoutly deny that all forces are resolvable into motion; and support themselves by such strong arguments as Prof. Birks, of Cambridge, England, has presented in his "Modern Physical Fatalism."

But all theory apart — whatever may be thought of the nature of force and of its origin, there can be no doubt that the whole amount of it involved in producing the ceaseless and universal deluge of change, and of stress towards change, that momently sweeps round this world and all worlds must be inconceivably great. Great results must have correspondingly great causes. Results infinitely extended in space and time bespeak an infinite sum of force.

But perhaps the justest impression of the astronomical dynamics is gained, not by considering how much the individual jets of force everywhere must sum up to, without regard to the magnitude of any one, but by looking at some of the larger exhibitions of that force here and elsewhere.

Look at our planet. What an idea of *power* is given in the rushing of winds, the tossing of oceans, the uplift of earthquakes, the thunder, lightning, and amazing velocity of electric discharges! Look through the geologic domain and see how the rocks have been melted, the strata broken and twisted and tilted and lifted as so many straws, lofty mountains and huge continents heaved up from the ocean bottom! What stormy heats and mighty vapors and gases wrestle and rave and heave away in the fiery heart of the earth and voice themselves in its volcanoes! What conflagrations, detonations, deluges, gigantic monsters terrible to behold, have left tokens of themselves! At any given moment what power is expressed in the aggregate of chemical actions, of vegetable processes, of animal processes and actions through all the populous seas and airs and lands! Looking only at the will-force (the force that obeys the summons of the will) put forth by all the animal tribes, and especially by man, and still more especially by the most forceful and executive of men, we find ourselves before a most impressive fact. The earth is alive with forces; not an atom but is energetically acting on all its fellow-atoms in many different ways; a vast hive of sleepless, bewildering dynamics, effervescing, swirling, "toiling and moiling" in every possible direction and with apparently endless mutual antagonisms, and yet somehow giving as their last result a scene of order and beauty and majesty. In short, the planet quivers and boils and surges with force at every point. The great furnace and crucible are never at rest. Who can sum up this mass of energy and state the confounding total?

Next look at the solar system. Here we have some hundreds of worlds, each of which resembles the earth in being a compact nest of domestic forces, and whose central orb indeed seems in many respects the theatre of a still more stormy and terrible energy. With what momentum the planets spin on their axes, with what independent momentum they swing about the sun, we have already seen. To these momenta add that with which the whole system whirls about yonder stellar centre, and so proceed to one knows not how many other momenta, till we reach the last great circuit of all. Do the same for every other planet system. Then sum up all these steady and swift careers and ask what measures of force they represent. What measure would a single person have to put forth in order to roll and swing all the immense masses of matter with so many distinct and amazing velocities about their innumerable centres?—this is really the question. And there is only one word that answers it. Infinite, says our struggling and vanquished arithmetic. Infinite, say our struggling and vanquished imaginations. Whatever our theory as to the nature and source of force—whether we view it as eternal motion or as something lying back of motion and producing it or tending to produce it; whether as exclusively the property of Deity, or as inhering in all mind and matter, or as belonging to matter only—there can be but one view taken of its dimensions as a sum total. They are unspeakable. They are awful. There is no natural idea connected with our astronomy, fruitful as it is in great ideas, which is more sublime than that of the astronomical forces regarded as a unit. And yet if these forces are secondary altogether, and the true scientist is obliged to add to them as their producers and controllers the forces of an Almighty Person, he is raised to a still loftier and vaster conception of the universe as a force. And this is my conception. I know myself to be an original, free, and separate force. I have good reason for thinking that all men, as well as other voluntary beings, are as much original agents (originators of motion or tendency to motion) as I am myself. This gives us a vast multitude of second causes or forces; and since phenomena also seem to flow from inanimate things as original sources, and as no positive ground for objecting to this seeming appears, I am disposed to make my list of original finite causes or agents infinite. But these causes are themselves both caused and governed by a First Cause who, from the nature of the case, is infinitely greater as a force than anything he has made. And if the total of creature-forces revealed in our astronomy is so wonderful in number, variety, and hugeness, how much more wonderful must be that creating and controlling force! We call it Almighty. It is worthy of the name.

XVI. POPULATIONS.

1. EARTH.
2. MARS.
3. OTHER PLANETS.
4. STELLAR REGIONS.
5. CONTRASTED VIEWS.
6. "MANY MANSIONS."
7. THE CENSUS.

XVI. POPULATIONS.

"For what purpose," says Sir John Herschel, "are we to suppose such magnificent bodies scattered through the abyss of space? Surely not to illumine our nights, which an additional moon of the thousandth part of our own world would do much better; not to sparkle as a pageant void of meaning and reality and to bewilder us among vain conjectures. Useful, it is true, they are to man as points of exact and permanent reference; but he must have studied astronomy to little purpose who can suppose man to be the only object of his Creator's care, or who does not see in the vast and wonderful apparatus around us provision for other races of animated beings."

How populous our earth is with both vegetable and animal life has been signally shown in the progress of modern research. We find the air, the lands, the waters swarming with incalculable multitudes and varieties of brute life. And over all the swarming hosts, down through microscopic nations of inconceivable smallness, rule some 1,400,000,000 of human beings. Our part of the heavens is wonderfully inhabited.

How is it with the parts that look down upon

us from the sky? Our telescopes do not yet enable us to answer this question directly, for they are not yet powerful enough to bring into view living beings or their works (if such exist) on even the nearest of the heavenly bodies. Still we are not without gleams of information.

Notice the planet Mars. This world resembles the earth so closely in regard to main habitable conditions that most creatures living here could live about equally well there. Land, water, and air, clouds, rains, and snows, continents, mountains, and plains, oceans, lakes, and rivers, day, night, and mean temperature answering to our own—Mars is really another earth, only on a somewhat smaller scale and with longer seasons. There seems no reason why, if our animated tribes could be transferred to that next-door neighbor of ours, nearly all of them could not have habitats assigned to them that would agree very well with those they now occupy. When we cousider the amazing abundance of life with us, how every nook and corner of available field is, so to speak, seized upon and economized for the production and support of animated beings, how, at every shadow of opportunity, as it were, nature bursts forth like the waters of the Deluge in irresistible torrents of organic being, we cannot easily resist the pressure on us to believe that she uses her equal opportunities on Mars with equal promptness and freedom. Here what would seem most unlikely places are packed with life almost to repletion. We can hardly individualize a cubic inch of air or water or dust anywhere without finding it expand under our glasses into a populous empire. It looks as if an all-observing eye had been narrowly watching for an opportunity to edge in and wedge in as many living organisms as possible. In short, our uniform experience in this world is to the effect that where life *can* be life is. So that one would have to resist the whole current of analogical inference, and the natural trend of thought and spontaneous logic, who, looking on such a beautiful globe of Mars as artists now fashion for us, and then mentally adding to it, one after another, the old rotation and the old cloud-laden atmosphere, and all the other old terrestrial facts which the telescope and spectroscope have warranted us in adding, until we see almost a perfect duplicate of our world as to main points, should refuse to complete the resemblance to our earth by adding a vast and varied population. It may well be doubted whether any well-balanced and unsophisticated mind ever did this. For myself, I should be disappointed if, on landing in Mars, I should not find there the equivalents of men.

Almost as much can reasonably be said as to the planet Venus. What of the other planets of our system? Must not their condition as to light and temperature, to say nothing of other matters, be such as to make life on them impossible? Think of Neptune, at whose distance the sun is only a star. Think of Mercury, to which the sun is sometimes ten times as large as it is to us. Yes; but then the temperature of a planet and the amount of light it has do not depend on the sun-distance alone; they depend also much on the sort and depth of atmosphere the planet has, its condition as to clouds, the nature of its soil, and especially its condition as to internal fires. By changing the condition of the earth as to these matters, as we may suppose it to be changed, we could easily raise or depress its temperature and measure of light to almost any extent. By enlarging the pupil of the eye we could see as well with the light of Uranus, which, under the earth-conditions, is nearly that of a thousand moons at the full, as we do now; or, by contracting it to a tenth of its present size the visual brilliancy at Mercury would be reduced to that at the earth. So every planet in the system, for aught that appears to the contrary, might be furnished with a climate and light suited to the terrestrial races. Some of these races are even now thriving in places as much without air and water as the moon need be supposed to be, in cold and darkness hardly less profound than is commonly supposed to belong to Neptune, in a heat and light hardly less intense than is commonly supposed to belong to Mercury.

But why speak of *terrestrial* races—as if there could be no other forms of living being than such as are found in our world! Who has a right to say either that God could not, or that he would not, make beings adapted to live and thrive in widely different physical conditions from our own! Must all his living creatures be made after the earthly patterns? Has the Omniscient and the Almighty such poverty of resources? Can he not make races that can live and flourish in the airless and waterless moon as well as we do here—as well even in the furnace of the sun, with its thousands of blazing equators, as we on our temperate zones? Could he not people worlds with pure spirits of any grade, which, from their very nature, would be independent of climate and other physical conditions? Could he not people them with beings whose ethereal bodies so closely border on the spiritual as to be almost independent of material surroundings? Nay, could he not so fashion and temper such gross materials as compose our own bodies as to suit them to a vigorous and enjoyable life in worlds vastly different from our own and in which we would immediately perish? Why could not an Infinite Being give as large a variety in physical life as in cosmical conditions: why is not the one field as large and as open to him as the other? Certainly, *a priori*, there is nothing in diversity of cosmical circumstances to hinder our believing that other worlds are abodes of living beings.

Notice under what widely different conditions life exists on the earth. It is found at the bottom of the ocean under almost infinite tons of pressure and with no appreciable light or air. Some animals must live in the air only, others in the water only, still others in both air and water. Some cannot live in the heat, and some cannot live in the cold; some can hardly have too much light, nor others too much darkness. Fluctuations of temperature that would destroy some plants and animals give vigor and stature and hardihood to others. Tropical life basks deliciously in sunbeams that would kill outright the Arctic; and Arctic fauna disport amid snows and ices and cutting blasts that would thrill the children of the equator into stone. Things that are poison to some forms of life are nourishing and necessary food to others. Minute animals are found thriving in strong acids that would instantly kill and consume many similar organisms. That quiet of the elements that is essential to the enjoyment, and even existence, of some animals must become tumults and wrestlings and storms to suit the taste and even the needs of others. The exhalations and gases that debilitate and annihilate one species are the very breath of life to another. Of late years we have been surprised to find how great a heat many microscopic eggs and seeds will bear without losing what is called their vitality—a fact very suggestive of what real vitality may sustain. The fable of the incombustible salamander finds much in actual fact to keep it in countenance. The three Hebrews walked unharmed in the midst of furnace-fires by force of miracle; by force of natural structure and adaptation volcano-fish in countless numbers dwell close about the heart of furnaces a hundred-fold hotter. We even have examples of life sustained without food, without stomach or head or any other assignable member, and even without any structure at all.

What a wide variety of mutually contradictory and, to a first view, seemingly impossible conditions of life! Does this variety suddenly come to an end just where our vision happens to do so? Pray, what reason have we for supposing that the only possible forms of living being must be somewhat like those found in this world? It certainly would be very unwise in me to argue from what I cannot bear to what another cannot, or from what one species cannot bear to what other species cannot, or from what all the sorts of living beings on the earth cannot bear to what those in other worlds cannot. For one, I have no idea that this little earth has exhausted either the invention or the power of the Creator. Who, in view of the wonderful fertility of resource displayed here, would venture to say that it is impossible, or even unlikely, that Almighty God should organize living beings of a high order whose natural and most felicitous home would be in even the terrible glories of the sun? The same power that made the seven-fold furnace at Babylon for a time harmless to three men could easily made the thousand-fold furnace that heats and cheers our solar system a permanent home and brilliant paradise of enjoyment to other specially-organized beings. We may at least say that, in view of the scantiness of our knowledge as to the foundation mystery of both matter and spirit; in view of the revealed fact that there are bodiless spirits, and of the scientific fact that there are etherealized forms of matter that border on spirit; also in view of the immense surprises to which science now frequently treats us, showing what men have been wont to call the incredible and impossible as actual facts—I say, in view of such things, it would seem that no one has a right to affirm that any physical differences that may exist among the heavenly bodies interpose any shadow of objection to their being, every one of them, the homes of intelligent beings of even as high order as man. If there is any positive reason for thinking that they are, in general, such homes, there is nothing that we know about them, or are likely to know about them, to interpose a negative, however feeble. On the contrary, the fact that in no one of the innumerable earth-situations, as extreme and unlikely to support life as can exist on other planets as the result of sun-distance (for example, situations without air or water or light or perceptible heat), do we, so far as we have examined, fail to find a crowded life, invites us by a mighty induction to believe that the planets are peopled, and that a God of infinite resources shows as vast a variety in his living creatures as he does in his dead materialisms.

The same considerations of course apply to the other planetary systems belonging to the fixed stars. We know nothing of these systems save what the analogies of our own system suggest. But it is infinitely unlikely that among the countless millions of those far-away systems, with suns and general structure strongly resembling our own, there are not some, nay, very many, worlds whose physical conditions are substantially like those of this world and could sustain the same forms of life. As to the others, however widely they may differ from our home, the difference does not, considering what God is and what we see about us, put a straw of difficulty in the way of our admitting that they all mean inhabited worlds. The Infinite One can easily match the varied palaces by as varied populations. The look of our own world is that He not only can do it, but is likely to have done it. All the currents of terrestrial and astronomical analogy sweep our thought in that direction. Whatever reason there is for believing that stars mean as many groups of circling planets is good for believing that planets mean habitations.

I would not venture to say that all the orbs of space are *at present* occupied by living beings. Some of them may be only in course of preparation for such occupancy. Nor would I venture to say that there are not some orbs which will never be so occupied, but will serve merely as sources of light and heat and control to inhabited worlds. Such may be our sun and those other suns that we call the fixed stars. But that they all are not a sort of lord-mayor's show, not mere fireworks of the Almighty, not a mere empty pageant gotten up by an infinite showman on an infinite parade-ground to dazzle the eyes of men, but vast worlds created and maintained for the sake of the living beings to whom they furnish suitable homes, cannot reasonably be questioned by a Christian theist. He believes that God made all the worlds. He believes that God had an object in making them. And he learns from the Scriptures that this object, so far as our earth is concerned, was *population*. For *he made it to be inhabited*. How natural and matter of course to conclude that those other worlds out in space, so like our own, have a like object, especially when we find ourselves unable to conceive of any other object equally worthy. The living beings of the creation are plainly its noblest part; indeed, lifeless masses of matter, however great and wisely put together, belong to an unspeakably lower plane; it cannot but be that the vastly less worthy should be for the sake and service of the other. How unlikely that God has confined the nobler part of his creation to a world so inconsiderable and unelaborate as compared with many worlds, if not most! How much greater and grander is Saturn with its eight moons and wonderful rings! How much more brilliant the sky that arches the planets of some multiple star with its various hues! Most astronomers, not to say all, confess to the impression that our earth is one of the smallest and least favored in its outward furnishings of all the orbs of space. Certainly our sun, vast and bright as it is, is greatly outshone in size and beauty by hosts of other suns, and it is not unreasonable to infer that the trains of these monarchs and the armies which they rule are correspondingly superior. Would God be likely to stock to repletion with his choicest works this world and leave far grander spheres totally vacant of them? To suppose it would be repeating the old error of Ptolemy in supposing the earth to contain the pivot and throne of the material creation. If we make it the only inhabited world we make it the grandest and most pivotal world in all the universe of God, for it is both centre and circumference of the *living* universe of creatures.

If we suppose that the worlds at large are for living beings, and especially for intelligent and moral beings, we at once rise to a most glorious and awe-inspiring conception of God and his empire. What populations! What multitudinous subjects as we pass from planet to planet, from system to system, from firmament to firmament! We are confounded by the breadth and splendor of an empire whose smallest miracle is in its acreage. And if those innumerable populations culminate in innumerable sons, loyal and happy sons of God (as we cannot but hope they do from the fact that the great redemptive sacrifice was made in this world), what new and gorgeous splendors are added to the august scene and realm of the Eternal! On the other hand, if we suppose all the worlds save this vacant of population both now and for evermore—great lifeless wastes of materialism stretching away into the infinites—without intelligence, without goodness, without even happiness or the possibility of it, we are oppressed by a sense of boundless waste and inaptitude and failure. As we go outward among the worlds and find nothing but an archipelago of shining deserts uncheered by the presence of a single living thing, there gradually comes upon us the sense of a mighty abortion; behold infinite statues left in the rough, infinite foundations without superstructure, infinite ships rotting on the original tramways, infinite palaces fit for kings without a solitary inmate, infinite thrones and nobody to sit on them, infinite navies traversing the seas and never a soul on board! Who can believe it that believes in the doctrine of chances? Who can believe it that believes in a designing Maker? Nay, who can believe it that believes that the worlds were naturally evolved out of an undesigning fire-mist? For the same rigid and unalterable natural conditions and forces that, in the process of the ages, have given such a world as this with its crowded and wondrous life, must be presumed to reach at last the same issues on the same path all through the heavens. If our primal fire-mist was enforced by stress of its own blind potencies and laws from stage to stage of improvement till at last it flowered into Platos and Newtons, must not this be accepted as expressing the nature and history of the other fire-mists which have gradually worked their way up into suns and systems like our own? They are evidently at least *on their way* to organic life, if they have not yet arrived at that goal. Having got so far on a course like our own, they are bound to go farther, to go until at last, under the irresistible pressure of the blind excelsior principle within, they come out on the lofty summits of conscious, intelligent, and moral being. And if the living races on the earth have not yet reached the limit of their advance, but, as is claimed, are still being pushed upward by the blessed though blind instinct of improvement which hides in all matter, then we are bound to presume that in multitudes of the celestial orbs the process of improvement has advanced much farther than it has with us, and "survival of the fittest" or some other ancient and blind schoolmaster gives angels instead of men.

All this in the light of the fact that the Bible tells us of many living persons other than men. God's holy angels in endless hosts, and the spirits of saved men have their proper homes on glorious materialisms *somewhere* out yonder in the profound of space. And somewhere, too, in that mysterious beyond are found the homes of Satan, his evil angels, and the lost souls of dead men. Each class of abodes may consist of many worlds; each certainly contains a vast population.

"In my Father's house are many mansions." Why may not the scriptural heaven consist of many worlds, and some of these heavenly spheres be among those seen glittering on our nightly sky? Are they too far apart to allow of that close intercourse with one another which is essential to our idea of heaven? We have had within a few years some very instructive hints as to what is possible in the way of eliminating factors of space and time from human problems, and that without lending ear in the least to the marvels of clairvoyance. As we are transported from place to place on the wings of the wind; as we write and talk freely in a moment across continents; as, by means of a glass, we instantaneously project our gaze across whole universes of new space, we find it easy to imagine that even such spaces as part the stars from one another may be practically no intervals at all to a higher order of being than ourselves, or even to ourselves in a higher state. "There is nothing fleeter than light"—what scientific man dares to say that? Nothing in what we know of nature forbids a swiftness as much greater than that of light as that is greater than the swiftness of a bird. Just as a ship may outstrip vastly the waves of the sea which it traverses, so a spirit may vastly outstrip the light waves of the ether (if such is your theory) through which it cleaves its way. Angels may flash through stellar intervals as quickly and easily as we can step into our nearest neighbor's house; may see and hear and converse through such intervals by their own unaided senses better than we do by the aid of telescope, telegraph, and telephone across provinces or even across the street. So the "many mansions" of heaven may mean a multitude of inhabited worlds which for all purposes of visitation and fellowship are practically as near to one another as are the cities of the same country, or even as the contiguous homes of the same village. Nay, the Bible teaches that there ever has been, and now is, such a free passing to and fro between heaven and earth as is inconsistent with the idea that the space between is of much account as an obstruction. "Are they not all ministering spirits sent forth to minister to them who shall be heirs of salvation?"

The same tenor of argument that would lead us to expect living beings in distant worlds would lead us to expect at their head beings answering to man, that crown and fulfilment of animated nature in this world, that is to say, beings capable of knowing, honoring, and freely serving their Maker. The same reasons that led God to crown his work here with such beings would be likely to lead him to do the same yonder. And for one, I should be disappointed if, on being transferred to the region of any fixed star, I should not find it, not only with planets and the planets themselves populous with living beings, but also find these living beings presided over by some akin in their powers and possibilities to man. Especially should I be disappointed in not finding such higher life, or a course of preparation for it, in those more glorious and elaborate systems with their many-colored suns in the presence of which our solar system is quite insignificant. Nay, I should rather expect to find on those ampler and grander globes a still grander type of intelligent and moral being than appears here. So, no doubt, would any one moderately conversant with astronomical facts who should allow his thought to float freely along on the current of their hints, analogies, and verisimilitudes. That can have but one direction. It is towards a belief in a broad universe of highly-organized and moral intelligences. To think of passing planet after planet, system after system, firmament after firmament, without meeting anything better than solitudes or the voices of brutes! Both the nature within us and the nature without us look at us forbiddingly.

We certainly live in the midst of a grandly-peopled as well as grandly-constructed universe—whether we trust to the revelation that is both Scripture and science or to that evolution scheme that is neither. But who shall take the census of yon far-stretching heavens? What record-books could hold it or tongue utter it or thought think it? Do I mean *human* thought? O Gabriel, canst thou grasp that in the presence of which our figures grow pale? There is One who knows by name all the rank and file of the glittering hosts that make our astronomy—nay, all the rank and file of the living organisms that bloom or move on their crowded surfaces; but then his name is nothing less than Omniscience. Our thoughts labor, our thoughts falter, our thoughts fall by the way and lie gasping, exhausted, despairing on the very threshold of an attempt to find their way to the great total of even those enormous spheres which have rolled forth from the Creator's hand. Will they even dare to *look* towards such an undertaking as asks for each individual life on all these thronged and glittering homes! And yet men sometimes attack the impossible. Great problems that long seemed far beyond human power have been solved, so that at last our venturesomeness has become very great; and perhaps we may be allowed to fancy that some one may be found hardy enough to face and strain at even so great a problem as this: "How many are the subjects of Jehovah in all the worlds?" He bends away at his thinking; he tries to push outward the walls of his understanding and fancy; he invokes endless factors of time, patience, and zeal to plume his efforts to put a girdle of conception about the whole great universe of celestial populations. Does he succeed? Does he long dream of succeeding? Icarus mounts; but the suns are too strong for his wings of wax. He falls e'er he has well begun his journey. And not if he had worn the talaria of Iris or Hermes, not if the tornado pinions of Michael the prince had beat fire on his helmet and sandals, could he have gone on to complete the round of that sublime orbit, or even made any appreciable advance upon it. Nothing short of a divine wing can accomplish such a journey. That wing can at once flash a radiant path about the whole universe; nay, is itself broad enough to cover with its glowing canopy the entire unspeakable area of being from centre to circumference. Does not such a wing belong to him of whom it can truly be said, "He telleth the number of the stars; he calleth them all by their names," "Neither is there any creature that is not manifest in his sight; but all things are naked and opened to the eyes of him with whom we have to do"? So it seems that God knows not merely all the worlds, not merely all the living beings on all the worlds, but also all the circumstances and affairs of every individual of all these abysmal populations. So he is qualified to be what he is, viz., a universal Providence. But we, in our conscious nothingness in the presence of such knowledge, what can we do but exclaim with the sage and seer, "When I consider the heavens, the work of thy fingers, the moon and the stars which thou hast ordained, what is man that thou art mindful of him?"

Such a view of the grandeur of the peopled universe over which God presides is certainly well fitted to promote humility in us as being a very insignificant part of the whole. But does it follow, as some would have us think, that such a world as ours is relatively too trifling to receive such an outlay of divine attention as the Scriptures assert? Doubtless, if God were like man, there would be a difficulty here. With us diffusion, beyond a certain point, means lack of thoroughness. In grasping quantity we often sacrifice quality. We enlarge our farms and pauperize our farming. We undertake many sciences and become sciolists. We broaden our landscape and lose sight of its details. Such is man. If one has only a small quantity of gold it has to be spread out thin to cover a great surface. But what if there is no end to the precious metal? Do not let us commit the exceeding folly of applying human limitations to God. He is the Infinite, the Unconditioned. In thinking of what he can do we must altogether discount considerations of number and magnitude and distance. It is as easy for him to do for a million as for one, to do for the innumerable as for the million. The Being who with one hand sowed immensity with monster spheres, and with the other fashioned the exquisite microcosms of animalcules visible only in the most potent magnifier, is not one to whom our thought can say, "Thus far shalt thou come and no farther." Attending to us does not compel him to scant attention on Jupiter or Alcyone. While he is pouring out on this world a notice and supervision that neglect nothing, however small, he is such a Being that he can do the same with infinite ease on every one of the countless worlds that are gathered within the unutterable round of the Ultimate System. Instead of exclaiming, with look of perplexity and incredulity, "How can it be that this little earth has had so much attention from the Sovereign of such vast celestial empires!" we should exclaim, "What a glorious thing it is that a Being exists who does not have to neglect the small in order to attend to the great, who can look after the smallest interest on the least planet with as much ease and completeness as if that were the only object of his attention instead of sharing it with an infinite multitude, and who can not only pour himself out to any extent as a knowledge and power through all the realms of maxima and minima at one and the same moment, but whose nature includes a demonstration that such a feat, eternally repeated, would be no tax whatever on his resources!"

It is but scientific to remember how liable men must be to misjudge the measures of a Being whose plans have respect to so broad a universe. Ought one to pronounce with confidence on a matter of which he sees only some insignificant angle? Are we not used to saying that a judge must have faculty to look, and take time to look, at his cases on all sides? But how shall a man look at all sides of a measure of an infinite administration, every act of which is taken with reference to every possible interest in space and time?

Are you tempted to think, with a certain Spanish Alphonso, that if you had been present at the creation you could have suggested an improvement?—that it would have been better if God had been revealed to us daily in a visible personal form of transcendent glory; that it would have been better to have no moral system at all than one including the present amount of sin and suffering; that it would have been better if the arts and sciences which have come to us so slowly and laboriously had been given complete to the race at its outset by direct revelation; that it would have been better if this or that feature of the Bible had been omitted or modified; that it would have been better if angels rather than men had been employed as heralds of the gospel; that it would have been better if further information had been given us about the future state, the mysteries of free-will and divine foreknowledge and foreordination, the origin of moral evil, the reconciliation of prayer with law and of religion with science? Take thought for a moment.

Think how measures of legislation that bear hard on one part of a country are often found salutary, and even essential, to the great country as a whole. Think how punishments that sacrifice the individual are essential to the salvation of society. Think how in all the walks of business partial and temporary ills have to be accepted as the conditions of large and final success; and of what our experience teaches us as to the necessity of general laws and of some incidental evils. Especially think how nothing is more common than for that which at first seems adverse or wrong to prove in course of time to be neither, but to be even disguised prosperity and righteousness. And then think how unspeakably vast is that empire of God to all parts of which his arrangements must have wise respect, and how impossible it must be for such faculties as ours to grasp them in all their bearings so as to see for ourselves their propriety. The best God can do for us is to affirm this propriety, and ask us to put faith in the affirmation. We should say to ourselves, "It cannot but be that God's management of so vast a scheme of things should sometimes seem to us not merely obscure, but even positively unwise and unrighteous. We must count on now and then finding laws which through our gimlet-holes of vision seem unwholesome, providences that seem the reverse of just and loving, doctrines that seem to frown on reason and truth." It will not always be so. All the great things belonging to this wide divine administration will not be made mysterious or wrong-looking by our extremely fractional view of them. Far from it. A golden shield, however vast its orb, will seem golden at many points to a sound eye. The fractions of the divine government that we see are often (may I not say generally?) as golden in their look as one could desire. But once in a while the eye falls on a spot where the light shines feebly, on a depression in the sculptured and pictured surface where shadows hide, on some ragged moon-edge where light and darkness contend together and which pricks our sight back into the arms of faith. And faith says, "It is only a *seeming*. If we could only see the matter on all sides and in all its bearings we should be quite satisfied. It belongs to an infinite scheme of wisdom and benevolence, and only seems unwise to us because we see only a small part of its relations. Trust the All-Father—*trust* him. It is necessary for little children to walk by faith in their parents. Would it not be preposterous for the little son of a great statesman (the child is only just beginning to walk and talk) to take it upon him to criticise the far-reaching plans and measures on which his father conducts the affairs of an empire? And must not the wisest and most salutary of these measures often seem otherwise to the little critic from his low standpoint, to such untaught eyes as his, and to eyes that can take in only so small a part of the circumstances of the case? With what modesty then should we, God's little ones, venture to pronounce on the ways of divine providence—on the statesmanship of that Father-King whose empire casts orbit about such an amazing sum of beings and interests!"

XVII. MYSTERIES.

1. SPACE.
2. DURATION.
3. SPIRIT.
4. MATTER.
5. FORCE.
6. ORGANISMS.
7. NATURE.
8. GOD.

MULTIPLE STARS.

 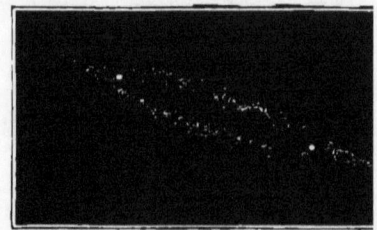

NUCLEATED NEBULÆ.

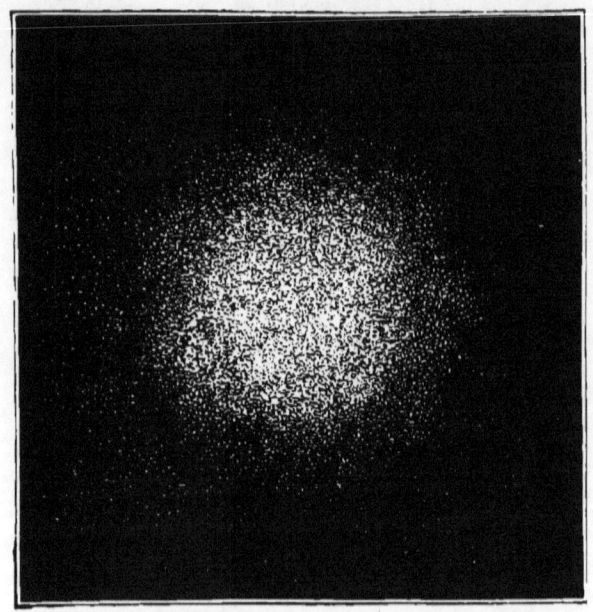

OMEGA CENTAURI, WITH COUNTLESS STARS.

XVII. MYSTERIES.

ONE of the most signal facts emphasized to us by the study of the astronomical universe is its *mysteriousness*. We stand, as it were, in the heart of an immense fog through which at great intervals a few strong lights succeed in struggling.

Of the things just about us we know only a very small part, and our knowledge of the things we are said to know is exceedingly fractional and superficial. Our intelligence is like a bird which alights on a twig here and there and picks up a seed. The nearest and most familiar thing we see has an unexplored interior which is the despair of our science. But as the distance of an object from us increases, the proportion of the known to the unknown rapidly diminishes. Whole estates, provinces, continents come to be hardly more than names. How little is known of Africa and the polar regions and the ocean depths and the deep interior of the planet! Our dredgings, the chippings and borings of our geologists, the corkscrew peerings of our microscopists, have merely crossed with a farthing candle the threshold of vast realms still buried in profound darkness. How little is understood of that familiar complex which we call the *weather*, or of that annual miracle of nature, restoration, which greets our eyes in the spring! It certainly is only an inappreciable fraction of our own planet that we can be said to know or to be able to know or to have any prospects of ever being able to know.

How much smaller a fraction of the truths contained in the solar system falls within the scope of our opportunity and intelligence! And as our thought goes out to still remoter systems, how dwindles the trifle at every step—much faster than the square of the distance increases—till at last we come to a profound of darkness unalleviated by a single ray! Is that star some 60,000 years of light-travel away? Yet still beyond may stretch infinite amplitudes of creation, unknown and, for the present at least, unknowable. On the whole, what we know are less than the stray sparks of a mighty conflagration. As a whole the universe is a Sphinx. Facts known are few; imaginations are more; the unimaginables are, beyond compare, the most. Such heights and depths of the unintelligible, such far-sweeping horizons and huge spheres of incomprehensibility, such ample field for even an immortality of lightning-eyed and lightning-paced investigation—there is at least one nebula that does not shine by its own light or by any other.

But let us look at this great mystery more closely. Space, the great astronomic theatre itself, the roomy region in which all the stars dwell and move, stretching away on all sides of us not only beyond any assignable limit, but into absolute endlessness, along whose diameter thought at its fleetest may fly for ever without once doubling on its track, is certainly a great mystery in itself. Who has mastered the idea of infinite, necessary space? It is an impregnable castle that defies all our philosophy. From the beginning giants have been beating and summoning at its barred gates and trying to scale its frowning walls of solid shadows and midnights, but the last man is just as far from success as was the first. By this time we ought to know and *do* know that its interior is hopelessly inaccessible to such minds as ours. That which is incontestably real, whose existence as a mighty fact forces itself, beyond the possibility of rejection, on the knowledge of all, but the nearest wall of which our intelligence has never passed and never can pass, certainly deserves to be called a mystery.

But our astronomy has as close relation to infinite duration as it has to infinite space. Infinite space itself inhabits eternity. The stars inhabit both of these shadowy mansions as nothing on the earth does. Each earthly thing, of course, exists in space and time; but how small a part of either does it occupy! Its place is but a point amid the endless regions about it, its time (that during which it remains the same thing) but a moment amid outlying eternities. But the stars occupy and reign in space and duration more largely and durably than any other objects of physical science. Even the soul of man is inferior in this respect; for though, in common with the stellar hosts, it may be expected to inherit all the future, it inhabits infinitely less than they of the past. For aught that appears, all space is populous with worlds; for aught that appears, there never has been and never will be a moment without the presence in it of created worlds. The uncreated and indestructible amphitheatre of duration in which the stars run their courses, and the absence of which is inconceivable, is equally august and infinite with that of space and equally unintelligible. They are twin mysteries—great cloudy homes within whose coincident and sublime architectures dwell all other mysteries, all created nature, and even the supernatural.

The contents of mysterious space and duration are partly matter. What is matter? We have our definitions of it, but they do not let us into the secret of its substance. Is it infinitely divisible?—a question often asked and never settled.

Of how many sorts is it? Once men said four; now they say more than sixty; by-and-by, perhaps, they will say more than a hundred, but more likely *one*. Matter was created, say we theits—something out of nothing. Here is a mystery. Matter was created, we say; but *when?* If any one can answer more definitely than the Bible does, *in the beginning*, he is more knowing than the rest of mankind. Was all matter created at one time, or did it appear at great intervals, and will there yet be creations from time to time? Has matter ever been annihilated? Some venture to say No; but they are either those who say that it has never been created, or they mean that it never ceases to be by means of natural forces and processes. Does GOD ever reduce matter to its primal nothingness? No answer.

In connection with matter we find a something easily seen to be much higher in its nature, around whose brightness even thicker veils seem to be drawn. I mean *spirit*, whether human or brutal. The last distinction between it and matter: its relation to form, size, space, organization; the tie that binds it to the body; their interactions; why the human spirit is not able to directly discern itself or discover its own exact situation in the body; the genesis of thought, feeling, choice; the philosophy of sleep and dreams; instincts, heredity; the metaphysics of free-will, responsibility, and immortality—all such matters, however speculated and dogmatized upon, suggest not only no end of hard questions, but no end of questions whose answers are as far beyond sight as is the remotest star.

Whether there are things besides matter and spirit that go to make up the substance of the universe, and if so, what and how many they are, who can tell? It certainly is possible that our present senses and consciousness cover only a small part of the constitution of nature. As there may be other kinds of matter than those at present known, as there may be other kinds of spirit than those we have happened to notice within our narrow beat, so there may be other kinds of substance than the spiritual and material, other kinds now known to higher natures than ours, or to ourselves when some dormant faculty shall awake and slip leashes. There is room for such discoveries in the great cosmos. Experience even seems to hint and feebly promise them. But they are Delphic promises—nebulæ whose interior no telescope can sound.

Force—what is it? The word is on the lips of all men; science just now swears by it; all nature is quick with the thing itself; some of its forms, laws, and relations are known; but who can be said to know the last essence of force? Despite the endless discussions from time out of mind, we cannot yet tell what that is in a thing which enables it to act on itself or something else—enables it to produce motion or tendency to motion, change or tendency to change—what it is and how it brings itself to bear on its object. We speak of chemical forces and vital forces, of the forces of gravity and electricity and magnetism and heat and spirit, indicating different classes of effects from which causes worthy of at least different names are inferred; but what that something is which is common to all these forces and makes them such, and what that is which discriminates the essence of one force from another, nobody knows, not even he who says that all force is motion and that various forces are only various modes of motion. Even he will be ready to admit that causation, especially on the astronomic field and in the endless intertwinings and entanglements and strifes of the celestial motions, is full of unresolvable problems. Can we answer such questions as one can ask about gravity? Does it act at infinite distance from its seat? Is a medium essential to its action on remote objects? Were a particle or a world created, would its attraction be felt *at once* in all parts of the universe? In whatever way such questions are viewed they cry mystery at both ears. There are mysteries enough in the doctrine of causation alone to keep scientific thought on the stretch till the day of judgment.

Ascending to the realm of the organic, we find ourselves in the presence of perhaps still profounder problems. Whatever we have learned of the structure and functions of vegetable and animal bodies still leaves them greatly in the dark. The mere words, *life, death, growth, reproduction*, what a nest and nexus of perplexities and impossible solutions do they suggest to us! Yet they stand for matters that have been in the focus of all eyes and thoughts from the beginning. The last foundations of heredity, the structural termini of species, stature, growth-period, and life, how wholly blind is our science as yet, and likely to be, in all such matters.

How many atoms compose the earth, in view of such facts as that a single grain of copper can be shown to be composed of at least 100,000,000 of atoms! To the infinite number making a globe 8,000 miles in diameter add as many infinites as there are globes in the whole heavens. Now you have a number which you can talk about and gather within the shining tentaculæ of poetical description; but as to any proper mental grasping of such an abyss of figures it cannot be done. So in looking at the sky we stand face to face with the mystery of incalculable and endless *number*.

This has already been incidentally noticed, as has also an equal mystery of size. On the earth we find things mysteriously small; in the heavens things mysteriously large. Here we have not merely inanimate atoms that are inconceivably minute, but also living beings furnished with all the organs of sense in the highest perfection and yet barely visible, as so organized, under a microscope magnifying 250,000 times. And how far may even these living infinitesimals be from the last minims of animated nature! On the other hand, peering up through the night, we discover a world to which our earth is almost a nothing—12,000,000,000 times greater—also a system of worlds within which could be packed away, at average star-distances from one another the cube of that number of such spheres; nay, a system that actually embraces within its glorious rotund the whole materialism and spiritualism of the universe. There is magnitude for you—a magnitude that is confounding, magnitude that is a mystery. Try your powers upon it and confess their inadequacy. You can do nothing. You are lost. Yet not more so than when, resigning telescope and telescopic imagination, you take up the microscope and, fancy-aided, carry your observation down among miracles of smallness. How far apart these extremes, both equally wonderful! On the one hand nature swelling into immeasurable hugeness, on the other dwindling into immeasurable littleness.

When the ancients wished to express a vast difference they said, *toto orbe*. But their orb was not much. We find in the astronomic field as now known to us a much stronger figure at our service. What an interval parts us from the nearest of the heavenly bodies! How much greater still the space between us and the nearest fixed star, and especially from the last star that appears in the field of the largest telescope! And yet what inexpressible distances beyond even that lie the frontiers of nature! We talk freely of such distances, but who of us understands them? We marshal long lines of figures whose unit itself is enormous beyond comprehension, and try by various comparisons to gain some faint conception of what the whole amounts to; but the baffling figures seem to laugh at and mock us as they stream away and at last disappear in the depths of distance and endless fog. No one has tried to give some just idea of the larger astronomical distances without feeling the utter inadequacy of speech or symbol to faithfully represent them. We are forced to content ourselves with some glittering generalities, with flashing out into the night some colored rocket of poetical description, and are glad of the momentary gleam, though it does make more sensible the greatness of the darkness. No doubt it will always be so. Thought in attempting to leap such chasms cannot but fall infinitely short of its mark, and so fall into an abyss of confusion. However far our science may advance and culture expand our powers they will still have to exclaim with astonished eyes and hands, and discouragement painted in every feature, Oh, those mysterious distances!

The simple transfer of an object from one place to another by a physical agent in immediate connection with it is not commonly thought to be mysterious. But when the motion takes place without any such agent, or without any sensible medium of connection with such agent; when the motion is seen to affect everything, so that there is not an atom of matter at absolute rest in all nature, or even at rest relatively to the other atoms of the same body, and even so that it is by no means the easiest thing in the world to disprove the hypothesis that every object, however dense and rigid it may seem, consists of atoms revolving in orbits about their common centre of gravity at intervals from one another relatively as great as those between the members of the solar system; when the motion is seen to be incessant as well as universal, and sometimes at the rate of more than 180,000 miles a second; when it means the transfer through space of huge worlds and huger systems of worlds at the rate of, say, from 50,000 to 1,200,000 miles an hour; when such a motion as this is combined with a thousand other motions woven together inextricably and yet never interfering with one another and separately calculable, as when a moon moves on its axis, also around its planet, also around the sun, also around the sun's centre of revolution, and so on indefinitely; when each of these motions has superimposed on it myriads of other motions called *perturbations*, which struggle towards all points of the compass—we find ourselves as much lost in this vast wilderness of motions as ever was traveller in new lands or babes in a wood. So many questions can be asked about them that science cannot answer nor hope to answer. What endless mazes! How the shuttles fly through the heavens in all directions, weaving out, we know not how, law and order and stability! Who can disentangle the threads that make up the wondrous web? Where is Ariadne? Astronomy is helpless and hopeless in the presence of such labyrinths.

MYSTERIES.

As a consequence of these mysterious motions we have an incessant change going on in the aspect of the sky. A chart of the sky as the first terrestrial animals saw it would differ very considerably from one now made. Our earth has a constant movement of translation through space, so that the place which it now occupies it has never occupied before and will never occupy again. As much is true of every other heavenly body. So there is a gradual change in the positions of all the stars relative to one another, mysteriously less than one would expect, considering the enormousness of the celestial motions, but real and one that must at last tell on the general aspect of the sky. But from the nature of the case this change is infinitely beyond calculation. If we knew that gravity controlled all these movements the task would be hopeless; how much more when we do not know but that there are many other forces with different laws in operation. Individual items of this change we can perceive and measure; but the great sum total pours itself in such floods over the face of nature that we dare not venture to launch our exploring bark on anything but here and there a creek putting out from the great Atlantic.

How it happens that amid this bewildering maze of movements no collision has yet been noticed among the stars or seems to threaten—what natural arrangements, if any, perpetuate indefinitely the mazy systems that, with their vacuum centres and eccentric orbits and widely dissimilar planes and directions of revolution, defy the conditions of stable equilibrium in the solar system—who can tell? We may get some light on the matter in particular cases, but the whole problem is plainly so large as to forbid its solution by any finite powers.

Who can suppose that our infant science has done anything more than make a beginning, an insignificant beginning, on the great field of nature? Doubtless elements, forces, and laws far more numerous than those yet discovered hide behind various veils. As our pryings into the worlds just about us, and especially in new places, are constantly being rewarded by new discoveries, we have reason to think that if we could transfer ourselves to distant worlds we should repeat this experience after a still more brilliant fashion, and find whole kingdoms of knowledge of which we have not now the slightest inkling. As a man with three senses ought not to pronounce it incredible that there should be five senses revealing attributes in nature of which he knows nothing, so we with our five senses ought not to pronounce it incredible that there should be beings with ten senses, each as different from all its fellows as sight is from taste, and revealing quite new departments of the creation. Did the stars come to an end just where the naked eye ended its vision, or where halted the vision of any one of the long apostolic succession of improving telescopes up to the huge Rossian? What astronomer supposes that at last we have seen the last of the stars? And surely it is likely rather than otherwise that essential nature does not end just where our present powers of observing it happen to halt; likely rather than otherwise that a great realm of attributes, to which no man in the present life has the key, and whose name is therefore *mystery*, lies deep within the nature that we know.

What a world of exquisite contrivances and uses; what prodigal riches, beauties, and grandeurs; what earnest and delighted study of these things, and sacred pilgrimages from world to world by radiant intelligences for the purpose of such study, are in all probability, hidden away from us beyond yonder blue depths! As we are continually finding new uses in terrestrial objects, even in many which at first seemed most forbidding, and have been doing so for a long time, we cannot doubt that a great deep of such utilities still remains to be explored just about us! How much greater deeps must there be in the numberless other worlds, every one of which was made by a wise and benevolent God, and to every one of which our science is only a tangent! What stores of bright and precious things are ever coming forth in driblets from the bosom of the earth; and who doubts that these are mere hints and prophecies of what the earth contains, and that a genuine clairvoyance through the strata away to the earth's heart would reveal vaster stores of silver and gold and gems than ever shone in dreams or Arabian Nights! Among the innumerable stars, and their still more numerous attendant worlds, how much of such wealth lies in hiding—the stars from whose golden light sometimes comes to our spectroscopes the light of gold! We can only speak nebulously; but we more than suspect that as our eyes rest on the evening firmament there silently enters them the sheen of inestimable riches. Also the sheen of landscapes without, whose beauty and grandeur befit worlds where sin has never reigned and among which come and go bright-winged intelligences on such pilgrimages from the "many mansions" of the central heaven as we are told have often been made to our world. For we cannot think that our small world is the only one to receive such heavenly delegations, but on the contrary must be-

ULTERIOR SYSTEMS.

lieve that far and wide the celestial spaces are flashing with radiant forms hastening along on sublime voyages of discovery, and studying from world to world and from system to system the wondrous works and ways of God. Mysterious activities of mysterious populations among mysteries of power and wisdom!

We have our biographies of individuals and nations. Geologists undertake to give us a sort of biography of this globe itself. But what we actually secure in all such cases when sure of our facts (which is not as often as one could wish) are a few of the easier and more superficial particulars that go to make up history. What is recorded is as nothing to what is left unrecorded. Here and there a ray of light touches a hill-top, or we single out a star on the nearer outskirts of a nebula, or we pick up a stone or shell or seaweed that may serve as a sample of the contents of that "great and wide sea in which are things innumerable," but whose abysses our eyes never penetrate. This is all our terrestrial history amounts to. As to the celestial history we know still less. If a complete history of a thing is a full account of all that has befallen its parts from the beginning, and if we cannot give a full account of what has happened to a single atom for a single day, much less for what is practically an eternity, what a hopeless and unimaginable unknown to us must be the full history of a planetary system, and especially of that great system which embraces all nature! We cannot put girdle about such a volume even in fancy. It exists in the mind of God, written out fully, down to the smallest particle of punctuation; and doubtless each event, however trifling, has left some trace of itself in nature which an Infinite Being could read; but to such power as ours such a book of remembrance must ever be sealed with more than seven seals.

Imbedded in these mysteries of history, and indeed a part of them, are mysteries of holiness and happiness, of sin and sorrow, of heaven and hell. We know of vast cosmical populations which must have been made for the sake of their relations to happiness and goodness; we know that great numbers of these are perfectly good and happy (but perfection in such matters is itself a mystery to us), while others are correspondingly wretched and sinful. So much we know from Scripture. But Scripture leaves heavy veils still depending before the places where, the times when, the manner how, the proportions in which, the good and bad, the happy and unhappy, subsist. One can ask no end of questions about such matters to which no answer comes. So much is unknown that, doubtless, when we "fly away" from earth it will be to surprising revelations, and yet such revelations as will never exhaust the darkness on which they prey. It will always be like some far-off stellar nebula which opens more and more under successive improvements of the telescope, but which always retains a background of the unresolved.

The material universe is often called the book of nature. It is not only a book, but a history. It contains within its mighty lids an exact account of every event that has ever taken place from that remote time when, at the creative word, worlds began to be, down to the latest present. Nay, more, it contains, and will always contain, innumerable copies of each such event. There is no danger that the universe will not always retain ample materials for reconstructing a complete fac-simile of its whole past.

Of course every event in the history of this or any other world on which light rests sends off into space in all directions rays which only need to be focused by an eye in order to make visible pictures of itself. These rays will never cease to travel (such is the general astronomic thought), so that there will always be somewhere in the universe endless latent photographs of the event. Thus the scene of the terrestrial creation, bathed in the new light, at once sent off copies of itself towards all points of the compass, copies which have been flying ever since and are now on the outskirts of that great historic sphere which has no absolute outskirts; and an eye there gathering in the flying rays would, if sufficiently sensitive, see the scene as a present reality. After the lapse of ages would arrive at the same point on the wings of light the picture of a new geologic epoch; after still other ages the picture of Eden and our first parents; after still other ages the picture of Jesus on the cross; and between these would be constantly arriving intermediate scenes both great and small, each at its proper interval of time. If the observer should tire of waiting for great epochal events, say the *atonement*, for the sight of which the old saints so hungered and thirsted, he would only need to travel towards the earth in order to shorten the interval; and if he could flash in a moment through the whole mighty interval to the earth he would successively meet and accumulate into a moment images of all the light-touched events on the globe since its creation. Also, if he should wish to continue his examination of any particular event, he could do so by accompanying the light that reveals it at equal pace; or if he should wish to protract the interval between the arrival of any two events, he could do so to any extent by moving with the proper velocity in the same direction. Thus, in the infinite sphere of space that surrounds the earth the nearer regions are occupied by the light that contains potentially the story of the most recent events, the most remote regions by that which contains the story of the most remote events, and all the intermediate spaces by pictures potential of all intermediate events chronologically arranged. And the time will never come when these latent photographs will not be winging their way somewhere in the universe in just the same position relative to one another in space as are the events themselves in time. Every visible thing, down to the smallest, is there, and everything in just the order and interval of its sequence, and as many exact copies of the series as there are radii of the great sphere, less by one. Like the successive chapters of history, like the historic slabs of Babylonia laid up in the temple of Belus in due order, here are the annals of all time done into pictures; nothing neglected, however small, nothing omitted because too large, neither suppression nor misrepresentation of the facts; in short, the Bible of history without note or comment, for ever beyond the reach of tampering hands, a permanent thesaurus and book of reference as to all facts that have shone in the light of sun or star or other luminary.

These views are not new. But are there not many events which occur in the darkness, especially such as cannot bear the light? Are there not still others which shine, but whose rays are speedily intercepted on all sides by impervious media, as by the walls of windowless dungeons or encompassing strata of the earth? Also, are there not spirits and spiritual things, such as thoughts, feelings, purposes, character, which never directly reveal themselves by light, and from the nature of the case cannot? Will not all such things fail to get registered in nature's great house of records and universal archives? It may well be questioned whether there is any spiritual thing that does not so pulse on the materialism that closely hugs it on every side as to leave on it some characteristic impression of itself, as it may be questioned whether any event in the world of matter ever takes place in absolute darkness, or has its outward-going rays totally cut off by perfectly opaque substances. But, granting that such rayless events do occur in the world of matter, it seems plain that they must yet so record themselves in all directions in space by characteristic micrographs that they can well be understood from them by at least a divine mind. From the nature of the case they must all be faithful expressions of the source from which they come; like fresh coins, they must all bear a picture of the sovereign from whom they issue. No atom can change its position without affecting in some way its neighbor. And this amounts to saying that every such change has an endless series of consequences in both space and time. So there is everywhere a state of things somewhat different from what there would have been if that change had not occurred, and so a state of things from which the proper powers could infer the event which has impressed itself upon it. From the law of gravity it follows that no particle can undergo any change of place without somewhat altering its attraction on every other particle, always in degree and almost always in direction. But the attraction of gravitation is not the only means which a particle has for influencing other particles. It may act chemically on its immediate neighbors, and this action alters their relations somewhat both chemically and mechanically to *their* immediate neighbors, and so wavelets of influence and results go out indefinitely in every direction. At whatever point a wavelet is found it carries wrapped up in itself all the peculiarities, both essential and circumstantial, of the original cause, and the proper analytical powers could interpret the cause from the result with perfect accuracy and completeness, just as our feebler analysis can resolve a given planetary motion into the various individual motions that compose it, and refer each one to its own cause—this to the moon, that to Venus, another to Mars. Thus every event that occurs is itself a cause, casting off in every direction an infinite number of autographs, as it were, which, if studied under sufficient magnifiers, can be made to surrender every feature of the cause, however minute. As every man's handwriting has its peculiarity by which an expert can identify him; as every man's handwriting at a given time contains the whole story of those physical and spiritual conditions whose resultant at the time guided his pen, though the deciphering is too much for us, so every event is really a chirography in whose mazy strokes is accurately registered a full account of all the influences which have made it what it is.

Certainly the ongoings of all Nature for a single moment would overwhelm with their countless items the memory and comprehension of the most gifted scholar. How much more these ongoings from the beginning till now! How much more still the infinite *records* of these endless movements indelibly written in scientific cipher on all the broad face and profound heart of the creation—the lines crossed and recrossed, imposed and superimposed, woven and interwoven beyond all the interpreting powers of man for a single solid sentence of the mighty scripture, though we are able to make out here and there a letter and perchance a word which we call science. In the alcoves of this immense librarium, this interstellar Alexandrian that will never suffer arson, we linger and wonder, we glance along its mighty corridors to where the vista ends in a star; we gaze up its dizzy altitudes and stages where tomes rise o'er tomes, archives o'er archives without end. August Bibliotheca, hieroglyph, chronograph, MYSTERY! Will it ever cease to be such? When will you find a surer or a greater?

I have said that such an unsparing record as natural laws tend to make of all events is beyond the present deciphering of any man. Even the record of his own single life is beyond it; and is likely to be beyond any of his future powers, destined to endless expansion as they are. Nay, it is likely that it would not be *desirable* for a good man to read such a full record of his past if he could ever become capable of it—not desirable, say, for the thief becoming penitent on the cross to be obliged to face always and wherever he goes every mortifying particular of his guilt and shame, to find all nature indelibly scribbled over with the shameful story. "Oh, for some Lethe to roll oblivion over the scene! Oh, that Nature would be merciful and reverse her awful stylus on the too faithful page!" But Nature has no mercy. He must look to the Supernatural for that. God can both erase and prevent the gloomy inscriptions he so much dreads to meet; and it is to be hoped and believed that the All-Powerful will do as much for every penitent sinner. "Blessed is the man whose iniquity is *covered.*" Nature would be a great terror to us all, apart from a merciful God. It is a comfort to us to believe that there is a Force regnant among the unpitying natural forces which is able in the widest sense to "blot out our transgressions."

And this brings us face to face with the greatest of all mysteries.

Yes, the celestial spaces contain a greater mystery than any we have yet mentioned, viz., GOD. "This world embarrasses me," said Voltaire: "I cannot imagine how this clock exists, and not a clock-maker." Much more embarrassing is the great clock of all the heavens. It strikes the knell of atheism. Somewhere out in yonder sublime materialism in the midst of a still sublimer created spiritual realm for the sake of which the material was made, dwells a PERSON to whom belong the unfathomable mysteries of self-existence, trinity in unity, creative force, omnipotence and omniscience, and whose sceptre touches every atom and event in the universe. That such a Being *is*, we can understand, but who can understand such a Being? I lift up my hand to the glowing firmament, and challenge answer from every star. "Canst thou by searching find out God?" Is there no voice in all the populous heavens to cry back, "Yes"? And a voice does come to me: I cover my face as I listen. "Yes, I know Him. I have computed his eternity, I have sounded his knowledge and power, I have measured his goodness, I have bounded all his faculties north, south, east, and west, I have taken the altitude of his throne. Yes, I know him altogether." That voice thrills me through and through. Yes, Lord it is even so. There is One that can say even as much as this—it is THYSELF. But every creature, from brute to supreme archangel, is either dumb or says, "Touching the Almighty, we cannot find him out. His greatness is unsearchable." Back of all those bright-eyed myriads there is not a single finite intelligence whose still brighter eyes can find out the Almighty to perfection, or even do more than blink at the dazzling photosphere of this Mystery of mysteries.

XVIII. MISCELLANIES.

1. WONDERFUL FACTS.
2. NOT SUCH TO SOME.
3. HOW TO THE SIXTEENTH CENTURY.
4. "PUT YOURSELF IN HIS PLACE."
5. THE ELECTRIC CIRCUIT.
6. FURTHER DISCOVERIES.
7. HELPFUL TO RELIGION.
8. NOT FAITH-COMPELLING.
9. A SCIENTIFIC MILLENNIUM.

XVIII. MISCELLANIES.

1. It is not easy, and certainly it is not desirable, to wholly avoid speculation in setting forth the main astronomical facts. Every great fact carries with itself a group of other facts, as a sun does a group of planets. These satellite-truths may none of them appear so clearly as the primary; and some may be little more than guesses, and yet demand a sort of recognition from us as being on a level, in point of probability and authority, with the ordinary informations that must largely guide our lives. But they ought to be stated for what they are, and not for what they are not; they ought not to be set down as demonstrated science, or anything like it, but as being more or less probable inferences or suggestions of science. If any inference is merely conjectural, let it be so stated. If he *suspects* that the axis of the earth is changing, or that its rotation-period is lengthening, or that space is a plenum, or that among the estimates of famous men as to the heat of the sun, varying from 1,669 degrees Fahrenheit to more than 5,000,000 degrees, the largest estimate of Secchi is right, or that the solar heat is maintained by the fall of meteorites, or that the

sun will become an iceberg in 10,000,000 of years, or that it will gradually suck all the members of its system into itself and universal bonfire, or that life was introduced into this world by meteorites from other worlds, especially if he suspects that the doctrine of gravity is at fault in the lunar theory, let it be frankly stated as a mere suspicion. "He that hath a dream, let him tell it as a dream." Let him be careful not to tell it as science, or even as what will sooner or later turn out to be science. This law is often sinned against, notably in the case of the nebular hypothesis. It is an *hypothesis*, but one that is often represented by its friends as scientifically proven. That it has some plausibilities, that it harmonizes with some observed facts, may properly be claimed: but this is nothing more than may be claimed for many known fictions. There are many *per contras* to be taken into account, especially among the stellar systems; it is only when such things are defied or neglected that the nebular part, or any other part, of the evolution scheme appears "as well established as the Copernican theory." Has Virchow no warrant at all for saying that "evolution has no scientific basis"? Are Secchi and Pasteur and Beale and Lotze and Max Müller some three centuries behind the age in agreeing with him? Can we afford to put Agassiz out of the realm of science because he wrote: "The thing is a scientific blunder, untrue in its facts, unscientific in its method, and ruinous in its tendency"? Must we invite such men as Alexander Humboldt and Sir John Herschel and Hugh Miller and Sir David Brewster to step down and out from their place as conscript fathers and amphictyons of science because they did not accept the development hypothesis as being science? It is true that some of these men are not now living; but it is not long since they left us, and they were possessed of all the main facts on the subject now known. If the status of the question has altered at all since their day it has been to the discredit of evolution.

But the chief astronomical teachings are not speculations. Mathematics and observation, made potential by superb instruments, have with vast labor dug them out of the infinite quarry of unknown fact. Yet they might easily pass for fictions with the uninstructed because of their very hugeness and splendor in which they transcend even Oriental fiction. For a time some of them, in the earlier stages of wrestling inquiry, seemed even to scholars hardly more than fictions founded on fact, as we complacently style some of our histories. But great as is the main astronomical story, even to mystery, it is simple, sober, unexaggerated, proven truth, far beyond most other sciences. Those great numbers, distances, sizes, systems, motions, orbits, periods, forces, perturbations, however staggering and dazzling the figures and thoughts they suggest, are no poetical hyperboles for which apology needs to be made to common sense, and which we blush to air in the presence of calm-eyed science.

Our main astronomical facts have sometimes come to us singly; with long intervals between has star after star fallen to the earth. Then suddenly the sky has blazed showers of meteors with their long trails of glory. Such were the times of Kepler and Galileo and Newton. "And the stars rain their fire and the beautiful sing." But whether singly, as if wrested painfully out of the hands of reluctant nature, or in an outburst of starry groups and constellations, as if, casting stint and measure aside, she had become a largess-giving queen, they are illustrious discoveries appealing strongly to our sense of wonder.

2. Still they may not at first seem wonderful to some of us. Some of us are *used* to them. We have known them from childhood; parents have incidentally spoken of them; teachers and text-books have formally explained and inculcated; an occasional lecture or book has kept fresh the

school lessons; and the effect has been to blunt the edge of wonder. Whoever has seen the evening sky, beautiful and glorious as it is, every evening for 70 years is apt to see it without a ripple of emotion of any sort; it has very likely no more effect on him than does the roof of a barn enlivened with fireflies. So after a little the abundant Mosaic and Christian miracles lost much of their power to impress; men who at first trembled with awe soon learned to look on them with steady nerves and flinty hearts; and if they were matters of daily observation for a lifetime, they came to be but as the daily rising of the sun. Even so, it may be, familiarity with the astronomic marvels may have dulled in some of my readers the natural sense of their exceeding greatness, so that when fairly marshalled before them they do not dilate the eyes one bit or send a single thrill, not even as much as comes when the country militia pass in review with tramp and banner.

3. But what would be the astonishment of any of us if we could be suddenly brought for the *first time* face to face with the heavens as science now sees them? The pretelescopic men of more than 300 years ago were like Aristotle's subterranean men in regard to our astronomy; and though furnished with the largest faculties and used to the

grandest thoughts, would have been amazed perhaps to dumbness could they have been suddenly set on the lofty eminence from which we look forth so commandingly into the sky. They had not dreamed of such splendid sights, such magnificent scenery, such marshalled hosts of the beautiful and grand. They could not have imagined to themselves such geometrical precision of measurements, such unveiling of celestial landscapes, such stupendous numbers, distances, sizes, motions, forces, systems, populations. If on some morning the Nuncius Siderius of Galileo had come to them with its sheet expanded to many times its old size, and blazoned all over with the sober astronomy of to-day, they would have promptly rejected it as incredible and impossible. As it was, it was a hard and slow matter to credit even such alphabetical facts as the optic tube of the great Florentine actually put under their eye. So they persecuted him, not so much the ecclesiastics of the period as his brother scientists. So his brother scientists at first persecuted the celestial mathematics of Newton. What are now universally received as elementary principles, by which all things are tried in the courts of our science, had to make their way through dispute, obloquy, and battle with the professed friends of knowledge. How would they have flashed out their utter unbelief and scorn had the whole budget of the marvellous astronomy that we know been offered to their acceptance at once! But if at last convinced by overwhelming evidence that what had seemed stupendous fictions were simple facts without one iota of inflation or false color, they would have stood with bare brows, flushed cheeks, open mouths, and uplifted hands; perhaps would have done as some enthusiastic patriots have been known to do on the news of great and unexpected victories. Unexpected? Was not all Europe embattled against us—numbers, experience, veteran commanders, munitions of war, everything? And yet here are Montenotte and Millesimo and Lonato and Castiglione and Arcole and Rivoli and Lisonzo—all within a twelvemonth! It was intoxicating. Up rose the shouts on the banks of the Seine, loud rang the bells, red glowed the bonfires, high waved the banners, fast and far thundered the rejoicing cannon. Was ever such a time! Was ever such glory! Was ever such a Napoleon Buonaparte!

It is said that the neighbors of Friar Bacon were so wonder-smitten at the scientific feats he performed that he was forced to conceal many of his discoveries and marvels lest the people should think him in league with the devil. Much more would this prudent reticence have been forced upon him if he had found himself charged with such stores of startling novelties as are no longer novelties to astronomers.

4. "Put yourself in his place." We should try to put ourselves in the place of those ancient men and see our astronomy as through their eyes. Is this possible? See how absorbed they are in the acting or the story. You speak to them, they do not hear; you appeal to their eyes, they do not see. The fact is they are far away, buried amid the old centuries or the old countries, wrapped up in the scenes and fortunes, the doings and experiences, of other people. For the present they are leading the lives of others, thinking what they think, feeling what they feel, struggling in their struggles. For the time being the cobbler is a king, the poor man rich, the coward a hero, the child a man. Instead of its being an unusual thing for one to be able to put himself in the place of another and, as it were, look at things through another's eyes, it is as common as it is for one to have a faculty for getting interested in a story.

This faculty, so commonly possessed, let us put into exercise, and look at our great astronomical facts as some neophyte among the stars would look at them, or as would the men of the fourteenth century. Ah, how the skies brighten, expand, multiply, sweep away into beautiful and glorious infinity on all hands! Adieu, Seven Wonders of the world! Adieu, Munchausen and the Arabian Nights! Your wonders are tameness itself. We, lovers of the marvellous, pass them all by in favor of this stupendous astronomy before whose startling greatness all mere fable stands abashed, though it deals with magic and fairies and genii and even Jupiters.

5. Does anything stand absolutely alone? Do not all the arts and sciences touch one another, sympathize with one another? Are they not all linked together in many subtile forms of interdependence, somewhat as are the different members of the same body to make one organic whole? In feeding one we feed all; in lifting one we lift all; so we would naturally suppose that such great astronomical discoveries must have greatly stimulated every other department of knowledge. In point of fact they were so many thunder-claps and fire-bells. They said to sleeping minds everywhere, "AWAKE! See what can be done. If the barriers of nature can be broken through here, why not elsewhere?" So the students of nature were encouraged to launch boldly forth on voyages of discovery. As the success of Columbus set in motion the exploring fleets of half the world, so the successes of the Newtons and Her-

schels started up scientific adventurers on all hands and sent them forth to knock at a hundred gates of the unknown. Not a department of nature but got a louder summons to surrender; not a science but became emulous of its stirring sister, felt the inspiration of her great example. Indeed, astronomy has acted as midwife at the birth of most modern sciences. Some of them, as optics, the calculus, the science of probabilities, and other mathematical sciences, are hardly less than her own children. They began to be and have grown largely through the effort to solve celestial problems. Also, the effort to improve the telescope, and to make and improve other astronomical instruments (for example, those used for making exact measurements of the meridian, as well as of stellar intervals), has led to great improvements in the mechanic arts and in those mingled sciences and arts which wait so efficiently on our civilization. Photography, chronometry, microscopy, and most of the arts and sciences of observation have largely gained their skill by acting as handmaids to her and reverently carrying her queenly train. Sometimes they have only stood by holding by her skirts. Especially is this true of navigation, on which commerce and all the arts which trade nourishes so thoroughly depend. So astronomy, the most ancient and perfect of sciences, has made or oxygenated the blood away to the very tips of the fingers of that body which we call society. It has sent thrill and verve into all thought and into all forms of labor. In fact, all the arts and sciences hold one another by the hand, and the electricity that makes one leap thrills through the whole circuit.

6. Has the last word been spoken? Has astronomy gone the length of her tether? Has she exhausted her material? or, if that is not possible, has she come to barriers insurmountable by human faculties, and always saying, "I forbid thee"? At the point where we now stand must we fold our arms and say there is nothing further to be hoped for in this direction? The Lord wills it; henceforth we are destined to be only consumers of celestial knowledge, never producers; to be heirs of the past, never bequeathers to the future."

History is against it. "If, simply referring to the progress of science in our own times, we compare the imperfect physical knowledge of Robert Boyle, Gilbert, and Hales with that of the present day, and remember that every few years are characterized by an increasing rapidity of advance, we shall be better able to imagine the periodical and endless changes which all physical sciences are destined to undergo. What has been already perceived by no means exhausts that which is perceptible. New substances and new forces will be discovered."

These views of Humboldt will be accepted as foreshadowing the future of astronomy.

It was not so very long ago when it was felt in some quarters that about all that could reasonably be expected in the way of unearthing valuable works of ancient men had been done. "Are not the museums of Europe already full of exhumed statues, vases, arms, utensils? There is an end to such things, and we have about reached it." When lo, the Roman Catacombs with their 900 miles of Christian antiquities; Pompeii with its vivid pictures of early Cæsarian Italy; Nineveh creeping out of the mounds of Mosul into the British Museum; Mycenæ and Troy long doubted but at last appearing above ground to confound the doubters; the giant cities of Bashan; the remains of the Aztec civilization on this continent —never were richer contributions to archæology than have been made within a few years. And now we are almost disposed to believe that under the Red Sea, or high among the snows of Ararat, or deep within the mounds of Zoan, or under the prehistoric sites of Etruria and Latium and Hellas, as well as in the still unbroken depths of this western continent, lie buried archaic treasures equal if not superior to any yet discovered. We shall go on digging and collecting. We shall still find the long-buried works and civilizations of primitive peoples, just as we are now finding scattered through all the leading languages fragments of the one speech with which our race began, and just as we shall continue to find fossils of geologic ages long anterior to man. At last perhaps we shall have what will be to our present knowledge of the far geological past what the circumstantial history of a nation is to a bare list of its sovereigns.

So notwithstanding the vast and brilliant stores of astronomical knowledge already in our possession, we are not to suppose our mine exhausted, or that we have exhausted our means of working it. Antiquarians draw from a limited storehouse. Not so astronomers. Their field is absolutely inexhaustible. And their exploring powers were never in a more encouraged and adventurous state than now. Their number was never so large. Instruments of investigation were never so many and dynamical. The greater the capital the more rapid the accumulation. Somehow victories pave the way for victories. We conquer because we are in the habit of conquering. Wait a little and you will find the outposts of our astronomy far advanced. There will, of course, be intervals of rest. Interregnums will occur. After a bountiful harvest will come a non-producing season, perhaps a winter; after a rainy season a season of no rain. But there will be other rains, other harvests, other summers, other star-showers, other reigns, world without end. So lift up your heads, ye young star-gazers, who fear that the great men of the past have left nothing for you to conquer. Broad provinces, great cities, mighty kingdoms of celestial truth which the fathers never knew, are within reach of the children—waiting to be conquered, *wanting* to be conquered. Bestir yourselves. Help advance the advancing frontiers! Stand on the shoulders of your predecessors, and see farther than they! Pile Pelion on Ossa, Uraniberg on Uraniberg, Switzerland on Switzerland, orb on orb, until the heavens are scaled and taken! If you do not do it, somebody else will. Some plucky adventurer who never knows when he is defeated, and who has been brought up on the homely maxim that, "There are as good fish in the sea as ever were caught," will carry off the prizes which your faint-heartedness thought out of your reach.

What are these prizes? Well, I am almost afraid to guess in print—almost afraid to undertake the business of a prophet so long after the completion of the canon. But if you insist on the scientific uses of the imagination, and on my venturing on specifications as to our astronomical future, I will, modestly and with a slight quaver in my voice, proceed to the venture.

In due time we shall have telescopes, spectroscopes, and other instruments of observation in comparison with which our present best are but children's toys—perhaps instruments of quite a different sort and as far transcending these as these do the rude instruments of Tycho Brahé or Hipparchus. Then the physical condition of the planets of our system, instead of being inferred distantly from various circumstances, will become a matter of direct observation. New moons will make their appearance. One new planet, at least, will be conclusively found glowing between Mercury and the sun; and its name will be Vulcan. A new planet will be found darkling and seemingly freezing beyond the orbit of Neptune; and its name, despite its coldness, will be Pluto. I scorn to say that many a new asteroid will be found between Mars and Jupiter; this goes without saying, is what everybody knows. What everybody does not know is that our new magnifiers, which will have found out a way to enlarge the image of a heavenly body without diminishing its brightness, will show us on planets of our system cities, temples, palaces, and other large works of the people inhabiting them; nay, perhaps the very people themselves. Did not Sir David Brewster say, "When we compare the telescope in Newton's time with that of Sir William Herschel we need scarcely despair of discovering the structures erected by the inhabitants of the moon"? So the books (mine among the rest) will cease to argue the plurality of worlds. Some new scope, which we may as well name dynamiscope, will show us the elementary constitution of the cold planets as the spectroscope now shows that of incandescent suns, and will detect and interpret modifications made in reflected light by the nature of the soil, as well as by that of the atmosphere from which it last comes to us. The theory of the sun, of the comets, of an interplanetary ether now so disputed and disputable in some points, will clear up; and the guesses of our present text-books exchange their subjunctives for the indicatives of positive knowledge. The Calculus of Newton and Laplace will be greatly reinforced, perhaps an analysis altogether new will be thought out, one as much more powerful than our present as that is more powerful than the geometry of Euclid or common arithmetic. And then the problem of the stability of the solar system under the new conditions and disturbances which Lagrange did not consider will get new solution, and it will appear that there are other guarantees of permanent equilibrium than those we now know of. And perhaps that present despair of physical astronomy, viz., the problem of the three bodies, will find its master in the new Calculus.

We find that there is a mysterious sympathy between the spots on the sun and magnetic phenomena on the earth. This mystery will be cleared up, and other ties of interdependence between the members of the solar family will be brought to light. And it may be (this is said in a whisper and with half-shut eyes) that on the currents of energy that come and go between the planets according to fixed laws, like the trade currents in our atmosphere and oceans between different countries, we may be able to send, if not articulate speech, at least some other symbol of thought to our planetary neighbors, and finally come to establish an intelligent communication with them that owes nothing to spiritualism.

But will the solar system engross all the new discoveries? Will not a fresh bridge be thrown by our astronomical engineers across the void between us and the fixed stars? I think I see it— think I see it in those mightier mathematics and observing instruments just on the brink of construction. Science will go out over the vast and unquavering arches and will find new suns and a plenty of them. It will measure among them new distances and sizes with unheard-of accuracy. It will detect new motions, orbits, systems. Such additional evidence of the unseen stellar planets that we all believe in will be found in the perturbations of the stellar motions as will transform our faith to sight; nay, our wonder-telescope will catch actual sight of not a few of those satellite planets which have so long hid themselves in distance and in the effulgence of their primaries. Many of those primaries will take on sensible diameters as no one of them has yet done. Will not repulsive forces as well as attractive be discovered? At least the shining fringe of laws widely different from that of gravity will come into view. The theory of light itself will come to be better understood, not to say reconstructed; and that still mysterious thing will be found to contain in its varieties of quality, degree, color, and motion a grand addition to that alphabet of which the spectroscope has already furnished us a few letters—a larger Rosetta Stone by which we can interpret the stars as to their elements, states, motions, directions, and perhaps age, as we are yet far from being able to do.

And then the nebulæ. As our telescopes have

improved, many of these objects that were said by experts to have the "characteristics of irresolvability strongly marked," have been resolved into stars. This process, I suspect, will go on, and, as has been the case in the past, even nebulæ giving the gaseous spectrum will be individualized into stars—wholly gaseous it may be, though not necessarily so—until at last the notion that any of the nebulæ are continuous firemists, such as the atheists demand for the natural production of celestial systems, will quietly drop out of our astronomy. There will be no repentance, little or no confession of mistake. That would be beneath the dignity of current science, that never forgets to be infallible. The task of confession will be left to the frankness and humility of a later generation. It is far easier to confess by proxy than in person—to confess the mistakes of our ancestors than our own. So the great nebular mistake, like the Ptolemaic and many another, will by degrees be quietly ignored, and at last disappear from text-book and speech, till the time comes for its appearance in astronomical history as an illustration of Humboldt's saying, "All works treating of empirical knowledge and of the connection of natural laws and physical phenomena are subject to the most marked modifications in the lapse of short periods of time;

and those scientific works which have, to use a common expression, become *antiquated* by the acquisition of new funds of knowledge, are thus continually being consigned to oblivion as unreadable."

Has not photography some triumphs in store on the whole astronomic field—on the moon, on the planets, on sporadic stars, on the nebulæ? We shall make cumulative pictures of celestial objects; we shall illuminate these pictures wonderfully with electric light or with some *vril* as much more powerful than electricity as dynamite is more powerful than common powder, and then we will bring to bear upon them wonderful magnifiers that will bring out to view the minims of the photo. These are the minims of the objects pictured. For light is not like other artists, contenting itself with general resemblance and the larger features of an object, but paints into her pictures everything, the whole sum of details down to the last jot with inconceivable fidelity and delicacy of pencil. Brought to bear on such all-comprehending pictures, our future miscroscopes will be able to descry moons, planets, suns far too minute for direct vision—will be able to discover objects on them, as forests, rivers, buildings, animals, manlike beings, and even smaller things.

We can accumulate the impressions which light

makes. The photograph plate which refuses to give instantaneous picture will, if subjected to the action of light for a considerable time, give a strong one. The color of vegetables and men may be greatly changed by long exposure to the sun when a brief one produces no sensible effect. That is, there is a heaping up of effects individually insignificant till their sum becomes appreciable and even impressive. Can we not accumulate light itself as well as the impressions it makes? As it has been found possible to collect and store away electricity so as to secure almost any amount of it for electric work, so it seems possible to collect and store away the light that comes from any object, say a star, till we have it in sufficient measure to make a great impression on the eye, the telescope, the photometer, the spectroscope, the photographic plate; so that a star of the sixteenth magnitude may be examined as one of the first, and one of the first magnitude as a sun. This plainly would open the door for many discoveries. Light has still about it many mysteries awaiting solution, and some of them seem waiting very impatiently. Their knocking at our doors seems almost a threat of breaking through unless we open speedily.

7. Whatever may be thought of these *suggestions* (please notice that I do not call them *theories*

"as well established as the Copernican"), there can be no question but that astronomy is still coming, and coming brilliantly. So great a past argues a great future. And, for one, I anticipate that the discoveries of the future, like those of the past, will, when once fairly understood in all their bearings, help the doctrine of the supernatural and revealed religion. Each will be a new step added to that golden flight of steps by which rational thought climbs to better views of God and of the duty we owe to him. More and more the stars will be signal fires by which heaven communicates with earth—the beacons to warn men off the rocks of atheism, both theoretical and practical; the mathematics of Laplace to prove, with a broader and wiser interest than his, that the probability that the planetary motions originated in a common cause is two million times greater than that the sun will rise to-morrow.

The first crude impressions of a new science, or of a new chapter of a science, are apt to be misleading. "A little learning is a dangerous thing." This half-truth has had no small show of support in the history of knowledge. Infant geology and archæology seemed to fight against the Bible. So did the infant astronomy of more than three centuries ago. And every now and then some new *find* in the heavens has been caught at by the atheist as giving new countenance to the notion that blind force and law, instead of a personal Being, is the true maker and monarch of nature. We are not yet out of the woods of this sort of foolishness and abomination. The very vastness of the universe is still too often interposed as a shield between us and God, made to conceal his person, hide our responsibility, and protect agnosticism. But such abuses of science are most common in its earlier stages, while it is yet strange and nebulous to the thought. As it becomes familiar, and its surroundings and relations clear up, it is very apt to face about and become a witness and champion for God and religion. So runs our experience. We have found that all ways lead to Rome.

Such will continue to be our finding. Very likely some of the new celestial facts that are knocking at our doors will at first be taken by some as making against God and Christianity. But "time will bring its revenges." Fuller knowledge will discover a friend in the enemy, a defender in the assailant. Competent men will start up to brush away misunderstandings and perversions, to set the truth in a just light, to translate its strangeness into the language of religion and, perhaps, into the very gospel of Christ. It must be so. More astronomical discoveries must mean more light on the existence, power, and wisdom of God, on the magnificence of his empire, and on the impossibility that such an empire as this has been formed or maintained by mere unthinking natural force and law. It must be that the better we understand the book of nature the plainer will appear the concord between it and that other divine Book which we call the Bible.

Some ancients thought and said that the stars make music as they roll. And so they do.

> "In reason's ear they all rejoice
> And utter forth a glorious voice,
> For ever singing as they shine,
> The hand that made us is divine."

There is such a thing as the "music of the spheres," beautiful chords and concords, beautiful harmonies fit for the angels to listen to; I had almost said beautiful enough, when fairly drunk in, to do what old Timotheus and divine Cecilia are said to have done:

> "He raised a mortal to the skies, she drew an angel down."

I speak not chiefly of their harmonies with one another which are so evident and remarkable, and in virtue of which they thread their way among one another in ten thousand complicate movements from age to age without collision; but rather of those higher harmonies which obtain between them and the doctrines and spirit of religion. In my view what has been found out respecting the stars accords exquisitely with the idea of a creative, superintending, and infinite personal God. It shows in him such a magnificence of empire and of faculty as is in most eloquent and tuneful agreement with what one would expect, with what the soul of man craves and needs, and with what the Bible teaches. Nay, from the nature of the case, all genuine science must sympathize with, take part with, sing with genuine religion. If religion is divine, and nature is divinely constructed and superintended, it follows, not only that they can never contradict each other, but even that they must be mutually helpful. And what is science but a faithful transcript of nature? So every science and every sound addition to science, in its general influence and final result, tends to play into the hands of religion. The two friends undertake to introduce and vouch for each other. God explains nature and nature explains God. Key and lock, they suggest and require each other. Science is the natural food and atmosphere of devotion. All appearances to the contrary notwithstanding, it goes to nourish our moral natures, to tone and brace them up as by mountain airs, to set them by many a breeze and current towards harmony with all the laws of God, natural and revealed. That it does not always do this is plain. That it ought always to do it is at least equally plain. Unhealthy natures may refuse to be nourished, and even be sickened still more, by the best food. Determined oarsmen can manage to go against wind and current. Diseased ears may interpret the choicest music into discord. So it happens that some scientists make science the handmaid of atheism. And yet it is true that all the sciences and arts (for the arts are as much a transcript of nature as the sciences themselves) are the natural allies of theism and religion, and even will prove themselves in the end what the Jesuits profess themselves to be, viz., *the militia of Jesus Christ.*

On this point Agassiz has claims to be heard—Agassiz, who once said to a friend, "I will frankly tell you that my experience in prolonged scientific investigations convinces me that a belief in God—a God who is behind and within all the vanishing points of human knowledge—adds a wonderful stimulus to the man who attempts to penetrate into the regions of the unknown. Of myself I may say that I never make the preparations for penetrating into some small province of nature hitherto undiscovered without breathing a prayer to the Being who hides his secrets from me only to allure me graciously on to the unfolding of them."

So spake the sage. But

"There is a sort of men whose faith is all
  In their five fingers and what fingering brings,
With all beyond of wondrous great and small
  Unnamed, uncounted in their tale of things;
A race of blinkards who peruse the case
  And shell of life, but feel no soul behind,
And in the marshalled world can find a place
  For all things, only not the marshalling mind.
'T is strange, 't is sad; and yet why blame the mole
  For channelling earth? such earthy things are they,
E'en let them muster forth in blank array
Frames with no pictures, pictures with no soul.
  I, while this dædal dome o'erspans the sod,
  Will own the Builder's hand and worship God."

If I thought science inconsistent with religion I should not be the friend to science that I am. Religion is better than the grandest secular knowledge. If I must sacrifice one, it should not be the greater good. I should be extremely sorry for the necessity of parting with either Cæsar or Rome—an bound to turn every way to avoid it; but if there is no help for it and one must be given up, then let Cæsar go. Much as I love the man, I love my country more. Religion, and the foundation for it in God and the Bible, is my country, and must be conserved at all costs. The best interests of society, its character, happiness, and salvation, depend on it. This fact, indeed, shows that it cannot be inconsistent with real science; but if we must suppose the impossible, and must make a choice between the knowledge of the schools and religion, between nature and the supernatural, between the works of God and God himself, between the teachings of geology or astronomy and those of the Bible, the choice is soon made. It is better to be good than to be scientific, better to be happy than to be knowing. If knowledge means wickedness, then perish knowledge. If error means happiness and virtue—a reformed, blessed, and sanctified world—then let error live. Truth has no value save as it helps to virtue and enjoyment. Suppose it to be without these issues, and you suppose it to be mere rubbish. You may turn your back on it without offence, for it is no longer Her Majesty. "If ignorance is bliss, 't is folly to be wise," how much more if it is also virtue! All the natural sciences, including even magnificent astronomy, may endow me with their whole capital and income to the last farthing, and yet leave me a beggarly wretch; but with religion alone I have supreme and inalienable riches. So if I must elect between the two, it is foreordained what my choice will be. Let Hagar depart; the other has the promises. But I am thankful that the case is such that I can keep both; keep one as the natural handmaid of the other, welcome every promise of a brilliant to-morrow for science as so much promise for the future of her diviner sister.

> "Should science tell me that my faith in God
>   Is vain, since God is not, nor any need
>   Of him, then would I banish from my creed
> All science, and take lessons from the clod,
>   Which, dumb and dead, like Aaron's budded rod,
>   Blooms yet, by miracle, to flowery mead,
>   Where plain, as in the Holy Book, I read
> God's power and goodness written on the sod.
> Not thus has science taught my grateful soul,
>   By starry gleam or secret cell explored,
>   Nor bid me dash my faith against a stone.
> She buoys my faith on all the tides that roll,
>   And tells me if to loftier heights I soared,
>   In farthest skies I should find God alone."

8. Though I anticipate that our coming astronomy, like that of to-day, will tend to magnify God and favor religion, yet I do not anticipate anything so conclusive in its character as to *compel* faith in God and his Word. On the contrary, I am confident that however brilliant future discoveries may be, and however loudly they may speak of the Creator and our duty to him, their voice will not be loud enough to command the ears and enforce the faith of everybody. The past has taught us what the future will be. A brilliant series of Christian scientists, whose faith and devoutness have been fed by their inquiries into nature—men like Newton and Cuvier and Brew-

ster, the ornaments of human nature, the glory of science, and the children of God—illuminates the past. And this apostolic succession will doubtless continue. But then we must expect by the side of it, what has always been found hitherto, another apostolate of quite a different pattern. They too will be scientists, sometimes of large faculty and great knowledge and widely successful research. But they will be of still greater unbelief. Eyes wide open on nature, but shut and sealed on nature's God. Diligent students of phenomena, but oblivious of the phenomenon Christ. Prompt to allow all considerations that make against religion, as prompt to challenge all considerations that make for it. Taking kindly and even overflowingly to all hypotheses and notions that exclude God, but exacting as Euclid and death against everything that includes Him. Swift to believe in all natural marvels, occult forces of matter, and even the practical omnipotence and omniscience of the eternal atom, and scornfully refusing even to consider evidence from any quarter of creation and historic miracles and special providences and an eternal Person. Of course such men will be found hereafter as they have been found hitherto. There is no conceivable wonder on the earth or in the sky which that sort of unbelief cannot successfully defy. It could stand out against the full blaze of New Testament miracles as well as the unbelief of the Jews did. Not if, on some fair evening, the name of God should be found written in shining capitals on every world that comes into the field of the telescope; not if each world should blossom o'er all its mighty orb with golden lips chanting in glorious polyglot the Name that is above every name till the earth resounds through all its latitudes and longitudes—not even then would unbelief necessarily lose its power of stubborn and triumphant resistance.

The history of astronomy shows us two omnipotences—one that of God the creator, the other that of man in resisting evidence. We can resist any amount of evidence if our wills are only perverse enough. This is the explanation, and the only explanation, which Biblical principles allow of the madness of "an undevout astronomer."

Who was it said, It would do our men of science no harm to be soundly converted? No matter—it is true, whoever said it. And far more than this is true. Nothing else would so assure the future of knowledge, as well as of religion, as would the general regeneration of the human will and heart. The great thing needed is not greater genius nor better tools nor vaster libraries, nor more government patronage nor reconstructed universities, so much as that great moral change which revolutionizes the attitude of the soul to its Maker and disposes it to "think the thoughts of God after him." This will repel the false as well as the wicked. This will invite the true as well as the holy. This will give love of truth and upright ways of seeking it, will give clear eyes, just balances, and steady hands. So both the Pharisees and Sadducees of science will disappear. We shall be able to dispense with our bristling apologetics and "reconciliations," for then we shall have, what the almightiness of truth and free inquiry and the scientific method has never yet been able to give us, a complete deliverance from the oppositions of science, falsely so called. Science and religion will always say ay to each other in sublime reciprocity. And then we shall have a scientific as well as Christian millennium, discoveries falling among us as star-showers of unparalleled gorgeousness, as an hegira of constellations, as a New Jerusalem descending out of heaven from God and pointing to Him with all its glittering spires and with every lifted white finger of its white-robed citizens.

www.ingramcontent.com/pod-product-compliance
Lightning Source LLC
Chambersburg PA
CBHW031858220426
43663CB00006B/669